CONCILIUM

THEOLOGY IN THE AGE OF RENEWAL

CONCILIUM

CONCILIUM/VOL. 25

MORAL THEOLOGY

UNDERSTANDING
THE SIGNS
OF THE TIMES

edited by FRANZ BOCKLE

VOLUME 25

CONCILIUM
theology in the age of renewal

PAULIST PRESS
NEW YORK, N.Y. / GLEN ROCK, N.J.

PAULIST PRESS
EXECUTIVE OFFICES: 304 W. 58th Street, New York, N.Y. and 21 Harristown Road, Glen Rock, N.J.
Executive Publisher: John A. Carr, C.S.P.
Executive Manager: Alvin A. Illig, C.S.P.
Asst. Executive Manager: Thomas E. Comber, C.S.P.

EDITORIAL OFFICES: 304 W. 58th Street, New York, N.Y.
Editor: Kevin A. Lynch, C.S.P.
Managing Editor: Urban P. Intondi

Printed and bound in the United States of America by
The Colonial Press Inc., Clinton, Mass.

CONTENTS

PREFACE 1
    Franz Böckle/Bonn, W. Germany
    Translated by
    Theodore L. Westow

PART I

ARTICLES

DOES THE NEW TESTAMENT PROVIDE PRINCIPLES
FOR MODERN MORAL THEOLOGY? 9
    Josef Blank/Würzburg, W. Germany
    Translated by
    Theodore L. Westow

TOWARD A MORALITY BASED ON THE MEANING
OF HISTORY: THE CONDITION AND RENEWAL
OF MORAL THEOLOGY 23
    Ildefons Lobo, O.S.B./Prades, France
    Translated by
    Paul Burns

THE NATURAL LAW AND STATUTE
LAW: A LAWYER'S VIEW 47
    Peter Benenson/London, England

BEYOND NATURAL LAW AND POSITIVISM 59
    Heinz-Horst Schrey/Heidelberg, W. Germany
    Translated by
    Paul Burns

REFLECTIONS ON THE VIRTUE
OF TRUTHFULNESS 75
    Stanley Kutz, C.S.B./Toronto, Canada

COMMUNICATIONS MEDIA AT THE
SERVICE OF "GOOD MORALS" 83
Léonce Hamelin, O.F.M./Montreal, Canada
Translated by
Anthony M. Buono

PART II

BIBLIOGRAPHICAL SURVEY

SECULARISM AND CHRISTIAN ETHICS:
SOME TYPES AND SYMPTOMS 97
Coenraad van Ouwerkerk, C.SS.R./Wittem, Netherlands
Translated by
Paul Burns

PART III

DO-C DOCUMENTATION CONCILIUM
Office of the Executive Secretary
Nijmegen, Netherlands

SIGNS OF THE TIMES 143
M. C. Vanhengel, O.P./Nijmegen, Netherlands
J. Peters, O.C.D./Nijmegen, Netherlands
Translated by
Theodore L. Westow

CONFESSING THE FAITH IN ASIA TODAY 153
Matthew Chen, O.P./Hong Kong, China

PASTORAL WORK IN AMSTERDAM 161
Michael van Hulten/Amsterdam, Netherlands
Translated by
Paul Burns

BIOGRAPHICAL NOTES 167

PREFACE

Franz Böckle/*Bonn, W. Germany*

"To carry out this task the Church must continually examine the signs of the times and interpret them in the light of the Gospel." This demand of the *Pastoral Constitution on the Church in the Modern World* is particularly relevant for moral theology. Among these signs of the times is the importance attributed today everywhere to the data and principles provided by empirical sociology and, related to it, cultural anthropology.[1]

Modern thought is largely dominated by the physical sciences and sociology. Moral theology is particularly concerned with the question of "norms", so prominent in these sciences. The norms that prevail in various societies are among the most important subjects of social and ethical research. While extreme situation-ethics puts the individual as such in the center and sees a laudable expression of freedom in his futile rebellion against social conventional norms, cultural sociology begins again to bring out the importance of valid norms. In order to survive at all in society, man can only rise above the insecurity of his instincts by a cultural transformation of these instincts. "Norms" then become the most important means in a cultural system by which

---

[1] This Preface embodies the material for a chapter in the book, *Der Sinn von Evolution*, which will be published by Patmos, Düsseldorf, toward the end of this year.

1

man can overcome his congenital insecurity. But cultural sociology also shows that this security may be achieved by various systems. There are, for example, various ways in which man regulates sexual relationships rationally. And while the norms accepted by one system cannot be transferred at random to another, there is, nevertheless, a genuine development within each system (theory of social change). Historical changes do not simply mean arbitrariness. In any case, the validity of cultural norms and their relativity are not on the same level. Unquestioned validity does not imply universality.

These sociological data confront moral theology with a series of very grave questions. Two of these will be dealt with in this volume. *First of all,* the theologian will have to ask himself whether the way to overcome human insecurity, this being subject to others, implies primarily a system of norms for one's behavior. The question is put by the Evangelical Danish theologian, K. E. Løstrup, in his book, *Die ethische Forderung,*[2] and his answer is negative. He accepts the importance of social norms for morality but does not see in them the real solution for the problem of overcoming man's insecurity. The *real* solution, as given by the New Testament, lies in obeying the basic moral demand as expressed in the twofold command of love of God and neighbor. For Løstrup the concrete norms are but an emergency solution when man refuses to accept the basic moral demand. In this case they indicate certain limits to arbitrariness and violence; they are, as it were, emergency measures against sin. Hence, Christian morality demands more than a mere obedience to norms. In view of the importance of this opinion, I asked a Catholic exegete to cope with "the problem of 'ethical norms' in the New Testament".

Apart from this question of the function of norms, there is a *second* problem which concerns the variety and changeability of various systems of norms. Should moral theology in view of this fact emphasize the unchangeability of its norms or does it, too, admit of historical development? A Spanish Benedictine, Ildefons

---

[2] K. Løstrup, *Die ethische Forderung* (Tübingen, 1959).

Lobo, shows how precisely salvation history, when applied to moral theology, demands the recognition of an inherent dynamic aspect in Christian morality. This is indirectly linked with the question of natural law, which is dealt with in two contributions. An English Catholic layman, Peter Benenson, examines the basic relationship between natural law and positive law. He shows that the appeal to natural law in no way requires that it be considered historically static. The Evangelical theologian, H.-H. Schrey, also examines the aspect of law in positive law and provides an informative survey of the attempts made by present-day Protestant moralists to find a theological basis for law.

After the problem of the historical conditioning and changeability of moral norms dealt with by these three authors, we must inevitably turn to the question of how far the magisterium of the Church can lay down specific norms as always binding. The Church claims the right to interpret natural law authentically. What does that mean? Is such an interpretation irrevocable, infallible, or merely obligatory for the conscience because it derives from competent authority? All this can be found in textbooks, usually in a very general fashion and without any differentiation. Accordingly, I approached a number of qualified theologians to see whether they would write an article on what is meant by "authentic interpretation"? Apparently nobody wanted to burn his fingers, and the article that was promised fell out at the last minute.

Since, however, the question is now being discussed fruitfully within the Church, some kind of answer should be given. In principle we must say that no Catholic theologian doubts that the Church's infallibility also applies to *moral* truths. But there is controversy about the question whether and how far this infallibility applies to matters of *purely* natural law. J. David, S.J., holds[3] that the Church can indeed teach with dogmatic certainty that there is such a thing as natural law; she can also test whether

[3] J. David, *Theologische Brennpunkte* 6/7, "Neue Aspekte der kirchlichen Ehelehre" (Berken-Enkheim, 1966), p. 87.

a specific teaching of natural law is compatible with revelation; but when she gives further decisions about the content of this natural law, she can no longer claim infallibility. David obviously means here that the Church is not given the effective assistance of the Holy Spirit for the explicitation of data of natural law and philosophical ideas as such.

This does not satisfy G. Ermecke[4] who believes that a right understanding of natural law demands more. By natural law he understands a social factor as subject to responsibility. He refers to those assumptions without which "man cannot be, nor remain, 'man' in the society of his fellowmen". This definition of natural law seems right to me. The best way of understanding natural law is to take it as the inner content of any concrete regulation of law and morality. This content is only visible and tangible *in a concrete and positive regulation of law and morality*. Just as the soul and spirit of man only exist in the concrete fact of his body, so can the content of law, as if it were the soul of concrete law, only exist in the shape of a concrete regulation. Real, existing law must necessarily be positive. On the other hand, a positive regulation without any legal essence cannot qualify as "law". This legal essence lies in the value and dignity of the human person—i.e., *man's understanding of himself provides that basic inner assumption to which we give the name "natural law"*. "Natural law cannot stand on its own: its demands can only be derived from the concrete self-realization of man as a person, and can only be measured and judged by comparing its historical expressions." [5]

Since Catholic theology lives in the conviction that, in Christ, something decisive has been revealed to man about himself, the Church is committed to the true image of man in this world. She must make an important contribution to man's true understanding of himself. But this understanding does not thereby get detached from his historical conditioning. The history of the West

[4] G. Ermecke, "Die katholische Ehemoral," in *Theol. u. Glaubel* (1967), pp. 56-61.
[5] L. Weber, "Die katholische Ehemoral," in *Ehe und Familie im Aufbau der Pfarrgemeinde* (Seelsorge-Verlag, Herder: Vienna, 1965), p. 52.

is therefore not intelligible without the influence of the Gospel. The declaration of human rights today is, among other things, a result of this influence.

Insofar, then, as the concept of natural law is rooted in man's understanding of himself and the Church has something decisive to say about this image of man, the Church has a basic doctrinal competence with regard to natural law. In this sense natural law as a whole is the subject matter of her teaching. But we must not forget that this competence with regard to this subject matter (man's understanding of his existence) is by its very nature linked to its witness to the revelation and the consequences thereof. It does not lie in the rational study of man and his structures, whether this study is philosophy, psychology, sociology or biology.

Such obviously does not prevent the Church from assisting in this with her teaching and proclamation. Here we must distinguish, with L. M. Weber, "between the Word of God, as we meet it above all in the scriptures and the living witness of the Church, and those religious and moral insights which man acquires in the meaningful existence of his person and in his experience of those supra-individual structures of the world with which he is concerned in his concrete freedom".[6]

According to sound theology, we understand by infallibility of the magisterium that effective assistance of the Spirit who preserves the Church from definite error in the knowledge and proposition of unchangeable revealed truths. But this does not hold for the unfolding of natural knowledge as such. The Church enjoys this assistance of the Spirit, not in the concrete expression of that human understanding and insight which precede moral teaching, but in her faithfulness to the revealed will of God. Insofar as an authentic interpretation is nothing else than a direct explanation and application of a revealed truth, it would indirectly share in the finality and infallibility of this truth. Insofar as it rests on natural understanding, it has no such guarantee, but, like this understanding, is subject to historical change. Most

[6] *Ibid.*

theologians are therefore convinced that, for instance, moral instructions on birth control cannot claim any finality because they are quite definitely based on a philosophical interpretation of human sexuality.

Such interpretations certainly demand the utmost respect (religious obedience) but there is no intelligible necessity to consent. In any case, we cannot work with two different concepts of infallibility, whether we are dealing with statements that are historically out of date or with important postulates of the present. Here, too, a sober objectivity is the best way to arrive at the truth.

PART I
ARTICLES

Josef Blank/*Würzburg, W. Germany*

Does the New Testament Provide Principles for Modern Moral Theology?

This article tries to connect modern moral theology with the morality of the New Testament. If we want to find a solution for the problems involved, it will be more useful to point out what the problems are rather than offer facts that may be useful later on. The basic approach is that the enduring tension between the demands of scripture and the requirements of the present must be maintained to make any progress in this discussion. We must find a *via media* between legalism and that spontaneous discerning choice of Christian freedom which, according to St. Paul, was bequeathed to the Church.

I

THE QUESTION OF "NORMS"

"We speak of norms [Latin: *norma* = carpenter's square] in philosophy and theology when we refer to principles, phenomena, values or situations which are taken as decisive or authoritative with regard to an attitude or relationship" (J. T. Ramsey, "Normen," in *Rel. in Gesch. und Gegenw.* IV, col. 152). This definition is useful for a first explanation but, curiously, does not occur in jurisprudence, although the idea became probably important first of all in that field (cf. the use of the term *normae generales* in Canon Law) and, as morality became more and more legalistic and casuistic, penetrated into moral theology. Thomas Aquinas apparently does not yet know of this use of the term in moral theology. He speaks of rule (*regula*) and law (*lex*) and he investigates reasons (*ratio*), kinds (*species*), ends (*finis*) and, above all, *virtus,* the habit which in fact and by nature influences man's actions. Thus we read (*Summa Theol.,* Ia-IIae, q. 19, a. 19c): "That human reason is the rule of human will, by which its goodness is measured, is due to the eternal law that is the mind of God."

According to this text the *regula voluntatis,* the rule that determines the decision of the will in man's actions, is not simply a norm but human reason as such, which, in turn, finds its standards in the divine *ratio* itself and this in the sense of man being made in the image of God, as is clear from the quotation of Psalm 4, 6 which follows St. Thomas' argument. It is clear that in this perspective the concept of "norm" is but a derived one; for St. Thomas it is a name (*enuntiabile*) rather than the real thing (*res*). It expresses the mind of man as the standard by which he has to decide, and in this the human mind remains subject and related to the mind of God. As this insight becomes obscure and loses its practical relevance, so the concept of "norm" becomes more and more autonomous and is seen as a "fixed norm" in the formalistic sense, whether linked with an autonomous human mind or with a formal and juridical view of "divine authority". And so we already have here in a nutshell the development of the idea of "norms" as a mere expression of outward order, as a formal postulate of the mind in the sense Kant uses it, and also as implying the positivist arbitrariness and lack of understanding of an authority which merely exists to lay down the law. "Norm" then becomes a matter of "declaring" instead of "assimilating", and in modern times it has already been integrated in many kinds of positivism. Accordingly, when we approach the great ethical systems of the past (e.g., Plato, Aristotle, the Stoa and Thomas Aquinas) with this view of "norm", we approach them with an alien view since neither the Greek *aretè* nor the Latin *virtus* corresponds to "norms" in the modern sense. And so, neither can the biblical commandments be seen as "norms."

To this must be added that there is no such thing as abstract ethics. Every ethical system that provides understanding and guidance in the human situation has its own historical and so-ciological context and must be understood within that context. It is true that it is not a mere reflection of historical and social relationships, but its principles and values cannot be under-stood without the social substructure. "Ethos", "mores", morals are, as etymology shows, for a large part social factors, each with a long chain of sociological implications, and it is not easy to decide how far the communal existence has determined the main ideas of what should be done, and vice versa. Obviously there is here a constantly shifting relationship. If we want to understand the character and statements of an ethical system, we have to consider its historical and sociological origin, its anthropological status (what was man's "image" at that time?) and its basic prin-ciples. Ethics is always the interplay of all these factors. Seen in this light, the question of norms taken by itself is sheer ab-straction.

II

The Impossibility of Applying the Modern Concept of "Norms" to the Bible (Old and New Testament)

This is already clear in the Old Testament. In connection with the idea of "justice" (*zedaqah*) in the Old Testament, G. von Rad has said: "It has been the custom to interpret the meaning of "justice" as the well-being of man in relation to an absolute norm, as something legal, the norm for which lies in the absolute idea of justice. Thus there remained only the question about the norm itself as presented in the Old Testament. But, however care-fully it was examined, the Old Testament, curiously, provided no satisfying answer to this question. The reason was that the ques-tion was wrongly put and so there was nothing in the Old Testament that corresponded to this concept."[1] In the same way M. Noth showed in his essay on "The Laws of the Pentateuch, Their Presuppositions and Meaning"[2] that the laws of the Old Testament can only be understood in the context of all the factors that went into the making of Israel as the covenanted people of Yahweh. The laws have a meaning of their own as the concrete expression of the way of life implied in the covenant situation of the whole people of Israel. They meant at the same time to apply this covenant to their concrete existence as a life led under the lordship of Yahweh. In this sense one must see in the first commandment a "theological axiom", as K. Barth has said.[3] Without this theological basis one cannot speak of "moral norms" in the Old Testament. This is already obvious from the fact that the whole Pentateuch was understood as the Torah of Yahweh, his law and his guidance. As the pharisaic-rabbinical interpretation of the law shows, the decisive point was that in these commandments one was dealing with God and God's claims.

The same applies in principle to the New Testament. Here, too, the question about "ethical norms" is irrelevant if we understand thereby a series of moral precepts which are then detached as generally valid moral principles, seen apart from the background of the faith, and then erected into a New Testament ethical system with universally human implications. R. Schnackenburg rightly observes: "The unity of the religious and the moral cannot be torn apart anywhere in the New Testament."[4] This is best seen in the fact that there is no one overall principle for an ethical system of the New Testament. Ethics based on the kingdom of God, on the imitation of Christ, on love, on eschatology, on the community, on the Spirit (and the modern flattening-out of this into a "conviction" ethics)—all these views are as

---

[1] G. von Rad, *Theologie des Alten Testaments* I (Munich, 1958), p. 368.

[2] M. Noth, *Gesammelte Studien zum Alten Testament*. Theol. Bücherei, 6 (Munich, 1957), pp. 9-141.

[3] K. Barth, *Das erste Gebot als theologisches Axiom*. Theologische Fragen und Antworten (Zollikon, 1957), pp. 127-43.

[4] R. Schnackenburg, *Die sittliche Botschaft des Neuen Testaments* V (Munich, ²1962).

varied as they are justified, and yet none can be made absolute because they are all interconnected and accentuate one or other aspect of the ethos of the New Testament. They only prove the complexity of the ethics of the New Testament and how *different this situation is from legalism and ethical systematization.*

The ethics of the New Testament cannot ultimately be systematized, and for good reasons. To put it into the straightjacket of a system is to force it, and this will always end up in one or other form of legalism. One cannot sacrifice the theological character to the eschatological, nor the christological to the ecclesiological. From the point of view of content, love undoubtedly has a primacy here. When Matthew states (22, 40) with finality: "On these two commandments depend all the law and the prophets" (Mt. 22, 40; cf. Mt. 22, 34-40 and Mk. 12, 28-34), the commandment of love is clearly understood as a kind of "principle" [5] (as Paul does in Romans 13, 9). But what do we mean by "principle" when we apply it to love (*agape*)? It cannot be understood as "norm", or paradoxically, as Augustine did when he said that the measure of love is to love without measure. If, then, the kingdom of God, imitation, eschatology, christology, ecclesiology, Spirit, freedom and love all form inextricably the background of New Testament ethics, it is clear that, without taking all these aspects into consideration, one cannot speak of "moral norms" in the New Testament.

The earliest attempt to do this might be seen in the so-called *Haustafeln* (domestic or local "tables of law", like those of Moses) in Col. 3, 18—4, 1; Eph. 5, 22—6, 9; 1 Tim. 2, 1-15; 6, 1f.; Tit. 2, 1-10; 1 Pet. 2, 13—3, 9.[6] The pattern of these summaries,

[5] Cf. K. Barth, *Das Gesetzesverständnis des Evangelisten Matthäus. Überlieferung und Auslegung im Matthäus-Evangelium.* Wiss. Monographien zum Alten und Neuen Testament, 1 (Neukirchen, ²1961), p. 72; W. Trilling, *Das wahre Israel.* Ges. Stud. z. A. u. N. Test. 10 (Munich, 1964), p. 207: "By this very fact we have here a wholly new situation, a basically different understanding of law. 'Law' as an established power which claims obedience has been ousted from within, because love, by its very nature, can never be a 'law' in the sense in which the rabbinate understood it."
[6] Cf. Dibelius-Greeven, *Handbuch zum Neuen Testament 2. An die*

however, was borrowed from Hellenistic-Stoic and Jewish propaganda. "Their occurrence in the earliest Christian writings shows that early Christianity felt the need to adjust itself to the demands of everyday life. This need was not obvious, since Christianity, which presented itself to the world, especially the Greek world (1 Thess. 1, 9f.), as an eschatological message, could, if it so desired, dispense with any such basic statements in regard to the cultural units of family or nation or even to culture at large." [7]

To establish such an ethical summary on existing models was therefore indicated when Christians wanted to define their position in the world in a positive way for the future. Here two problems arose—that of establishing an ethic and that of adapting the eschatological aspect to the present. The Christian community had to face this problem in a way which went beyond the community and its authentic tradition wherever the relation to the surrounding society, within which the Church had to continue, demanded clarification. Hence the Christian ethic cannot escape the fact that it has to adjust itself to constantly changing relationships. This Christian ethic, of course, has definite basic attitudes and tendencies, but these are, on the whole, so open and flexible that they can meet any new demands and risk new expressions. On the whole, therefore, one has to agree with J. Leclercq: "We should underline more the essence of Christianity. It obviously *includes* a definite morality. . . . But Christianity *is not* just a morality; it is a religion." [8]

III

THE QUESTION OF INTERPRETATION

For present-day moral theologians, the main difficulty of New Testament morality lies in the question of how to interpret and

---

Kolosser, Epheser, An Philemon (Tübingen, ³1953): exc. "Haustafeln," pp. 48ff.

[7] *Loc. cit.*, p. 48.

[8] J. Leclercq, *Essais de Morale Catholique*. I: Le Retour à Jésus (Tournai/Paris, 1950), p. 25.

apply those New Testament texts that have a moral content. One cannot just ignore the difficulty of this problem. By the nature of his subject the moral theologian is confronted with modern problems and with the needs of modern man. He is and must be primarily concerned with the present, and he has to find an answer. He therefore expects some assistance from the exegetes. But when he turns to exegesis, the New Testament, or the bible as a whole, he is often disappointed. The historical method in exegesis has laid bare the historical conditions of the bible and the historical character of the biblical revelation, and this has produced a tension between the theological-canonical view of the bible as it was current in the recent past and the new realization of this historical character. To this must be added the treatment of the bible by *Formgeschichte* and the history of tradition and of the editing process, which complicate the approach to the apparently simple text of the bible so that, unless he is an exegete himself, the theologian will be afraid of what the professional will say.

Moreover, there is a lack of historical continuity of biblical interpretation in the Catholic tradition, such as exists in the Evangelical tradition. By this I mean that natural familiarity with the bible which allows one to think in biblical terms with an ease acquired by constant practice, even when one is dealing with moral or dogmatic theology and not with exegesis as such. With us the process is usually the other way around: we take pains not to force systematic ideas on the bible from elsewhere, whether old or new, since neither apply to the bible. One cannot deny that there is this gap between exegesis and the tradition of moral theology, and this fact must be frankly admitted if we want to solve the difficulty. All this gives us the impression that the bible belongs to a period that is historically alien to us; that it deals with ideas, images and presentations that have no meaning for us anymore; that the questions it considers are no longer our questions and that it provides no answer to these questions. If we ignore its historical character and take it as an independent and immediate authority, as the direct "Word of God", we gain nothing, since—apart from such general conceptions as the command of love—many statements stand, oddly isolated, in the middle of our present condition. And so, in one way or another, we cannot escape the question of interpretation (and here the "existential" interpretation is but *one, and not the only* answer!).

The exegete who establishes the purely historical and theological content of biblical statements and then presents them systematically is mistaken if he expects that his conclusions can be taken over just as they stand. As an historical conglomeration the bible remains alien to modern consciousness and is not really assimilated. In spite of all the efforts of contemporary exegesis, this remains the most difficult problem and one that is still far from being solved. On the other hand, it would also be wrong to project modern thoughts uncritically into the text of the bible. This difficulty is experienced in moral theology more than anywhere else because it is primarily concerned with the present. If, in the eyes of the exegete, moral theology is still lagging behind, it is principally due to this still unsolved problem of communication.

IV

SHOULD WE ADAPT OR OPPOSE?

The difficulty may be illustrated with two deliberately extreme examples, and start with the question: What can still appeal to man in this present society? Ephesians 5, 22-33 describes the marital relations between man and wife. "Wives, be subject to your husbands as to the Lord." The husband should "love his wife as himself", and the wife should "respect her husband". This, it is said, simply reflects a patriarchal situation which we have left behind long ago and no longer corresponds to the modern concept of equality of the sexes or the modern view of marriage as a partnership. If we add to this the peculiar reasons that Paul gives (1 Cor. 11, 2-16) for women wearing a veil, reasons that are no longer quite intelligible even to the expert exegete, and

look at that hierarchical arrangement: God is the head of Christ
—Christ the head of man—man the head of woman (1 Cor. 11, 3), we find that even with the best will in the world it is difficult to understand, although it obviously had theological importance for Paul. One can then maintain that the context immediately afterward (vv. 11-12) solves the problem by saying that "in the Lord" woman is not independent of man, or man independent of woman, and that as woman is "from the man", so man is "because of woman, but all is from God". But then we see in this passage that even in Paul two views or tendencies compete with each other and continue in this manner without solution. Thus we conclude that we must distinguish between what in Paul, and in the New Testament generally, is historically and sociologically conditioned, and what is valid in principle, even for today. This leads to a critical treatment of the matter, and for this we must find in the New Testament itself the criteria with which we can justify this distinction. This is not quite as new as it appears, since this has been done repeatedly in the course of the history of theology, as with the communion of the chalice.

But there is another type of argument. If we take the Sermon on the Mount (Mt. 5—7), we find that the traditional morality "on two levels" has worked out, hand in hand with the casuistry of the confessional, a Christian middle position that made the decalogue and the commandments of the Church obligatory but hardly tried to bring home the exhortations of the Sermon on the Mount. These, and a whole series of other exhortations, were considered to be reserved as "extraordinary" to those Christians who were not satisfied with what was generally prescribed and wanted to do something special. But should not all Christians take the exhortations of the New Testament seriously and practice them? Whenever Christianity has been taken seriously it has always cut across all ages and situations. There has never been a time in the Church, not even during the Middle Ages as we now know, when the dominant social morality was totally in agreement with the Christian ethos. The harmony between "nature" and "supernature" has never really existed except in the imagination of the theologians. As the saints have shown, it never existed in practice except as a very rare and fortunate coincidence. Should Christians not be the salt of the earth and query this taking for granted of compromise in a social situation that is by no means necessarily "good in itself"? And from where should one draw the courage to be different in the manner of that Christian non-conformity of Romans 12, 1-2, unless in this "alien" yet basically constructive morality of the New Testament, which can then remain continuous and undiminished in its validity? The Christian should first of all listen to God and Christ and seek to do God's will; in this he may be almost completely indifferent to the opinion of society, and he even ought to, or otherwise he will never start. If he does not want the whole of Christianity, he will have nothing.

There is undoubtedly some truth in both these arguments, and one cannot get out of the difficulty by playing off one against the other. This shows how little further we get with a legalistic approach which, in the past, was taken to produce a final and clear certainty. The classic morality on two levels tried to escape from the dilemma by taking the line of practical convenience, but paid for it by leveling all that is typically Christian. It was correctly seen that the Sermon on the Mount could not be turned into laws but was a matter of voluntary acceptance, with the understandable result that more attention was paid to what could be regulated by law. Nevertheless, in Matthew we read: "You, therefore, must be perfect, as your heavenly Father is perfect" (Mt. 5, 48; cf. Lk. 6, 36), and this applies to all believers. Yet, both of these apparently contradictory tendencies of standing open to as many as possible on the one hand and toward wholeness and perfection on the other must be brought together. Only the recognition of this "openness to all", even to the greatest sinners, saves Christian perfection from sliding into pharisaism, an elite system, a legal "highest productivity" morality, and so we shall remember that even the "perfect" Christian is a saved sinner. In the same way, only if we take the search for perfection seriously will we give ourselves to our brother, whatever his condition, with the authenticity and courage that are required if we really want to change evil situations without compromise. The sinner who repents and seeks compassion and the "righteous one" who lives in faith, hope and charity need each other in the Church, the one in order not to despair, the other also in order not to despair at the sight of so few true Christians.

V

ETHICAL PATTERNS

There are, particularly in the epistles, a number of exhortations where one has clearly to ask whether the sociological circumstances, valid at the time of writing, also apply to our circumstances. This holds especially for the social situation of those days (domestic situations, slavery, pagan idolatry with all its implications, relations with society and the State in the broadest sense). We should remember, however, that our present worldwide society is compacted of a constant interchange of other ages and that there may be many things that are just as actual today as they were in antiquity. Now, the Pauline epistles (genuine or not) often contain statements of theological principle, particularly in the matter of the motivation of these exhortations, and the question arises whether, with these concrete circumstances, the theological principles have also become obsolete. The best example is perhaps 1 Corinthians 8—10, the question of eating sacrificial meats and Christian participation in pagan banquets. As the matter is put there, the situation might still be actual in mission countries but certainly not in modern industrial society. But Paul links this question with a number of important theological observations on Christian freedom and its practice among the brethren. Paul says there that, for the sake of the weaker brother and out of respect for his conscience, we may be obliged to forego rights and liberties to which we are entitled (1 Cor. 8, 7-13). In Chapter 9 he illustrates this with his own case. As an apostle he has, for the sake of unhampered preaching and in order to become all things to all men (1 Cor. 9, 19-23), renounced certain privileges that custom entitles him to, such as being provided for by the community (a right traced back to the Lord: 1 Cor. 9, 14), as well as the right to marry which was without doubt exercised by the other apostles, Peter included (1 Cor. 9, 5). The proximate occasion of these remarks is undoubtedly out of date, both historically and sociologically, but this cannot be maintained in regard to what Paul says concerning Christian freedom and its practice in relation to the brethren. This is rather a characteristic of Christian morality and one of lasting importance. In the same way there are very many cases where one has to see whether, beyond the historical circumstances and instructions, there is not a deeper and characteristic point made, with some broader intention which can easily be applied to the present situation and seen to be relevant for modern problems. This does not eliminate the historical element, but we must examine the meaning which lies buried in what once happened but which points beyond the historical circumstances to future relevance.

Insofar as the exhortations of the gospels are concerned, particularly the Sermon on the Mount, we should remember that they belong to a literary genre and are verbal images rather than straightforward moral commandments. This shows, as has been already brought out by the history of their interpretation, that they are not to be treated in a legalistic manner. We have but to look at the older exegesis—particularly that around the turn of the 19th century, which tried to impose the casuistic norms of moral theology on the Sermon on the Mount—to see with what blunt instruments some people tried to hammer away at a futile object. The result was that they preferred to leave these exhortations alone or to abandon them to some vague meditation. Yet, these picturesque exhortations certainly aimed at deeds, and not merely pious thoughts; they are directed to man's will, but man himself has to discover the manner and degree of putting them into practice in a way that cannot be laid down by law beforehand. The action involved can only spring from freedom, faith,

restless love and eschatological hope in view of saving an un-
saved world. It can, therefore, only be realized in trust in Christ
crucified and risen, in the acceptance of the promise of his kingdom, and thus only in the sphere of christology and eschatology.

The apparently unrealistic attitude that makes one not resist
the evildoer, but allows the evil to work itself out (Mt. 5, 38-42),
or makes one try to overcome it through goodness (Rom. 13,
21), cannot be simply dismissed; it demands that "hope against
hope" of Romans 4, 17, or the "faith of Abraham". It is at this
point that the relevance of the faith in the world is decided, and
not in an uncritical acceptance of a situation. The Sermon on the
Mount must therefore be understood as a "striving", but not in a
fundamentalist or legalistic way. The attitude it demands is one
of nobility of soul, not that of the mean calculations of a spiritual
grocer or security official. It calls forth initiative and imagination and shrewd judgment of a situation, things that a morality
mainly concerned with goodness cannot do without, although
they are dangerous and superfluous for a morality that is desper-
ately nervous never to move in the wrong direction. Up until now
the attitude toward the Sermon on the Mount hovered between
legalism and irrelevance. What is important in it is the presenta-
tion of an ethos that binds without a law. This is precisely what
it set out to give. We have suffered too long from a mentality
which considered that anything that could not be regulated by
general prescription but had to be left to man's free will was
bound to go wrong. Jesus clearly thought differently. He expects
man to believe, and that means to trust.

Between a legalism with its absolute claims—which can only
lead to an absolutist practice and, with it, lack of freedom—on
the one hand, and the lack of all compulsion through indifference
and arbitrariness on the other, the problem of the historical
limitations of the New Testament (and therefore of the whole
moral theology since then) and the problem of interpretation
and application need the concept of "ethical patterns".[9] A "pat-

---

[9] I have taken over the concept of "Patterns" from T. W. Adorno,
Negative Dialektik (Frankfurt a. M., 1966), p. 37: "A binding force

tern", or, as Paul and the Fathers would say, a "type",[10] is at the same time something concrete and capable of adjustment. Insofar as it is definite and part of the historical revelation, the pattern would provide that "compulsion" implied in revelation, as we expect it from scripture; but at the same time, the fact that it is a "pattern" allows us to rethink its implications in a new interpretation for the present time. The morality of the New Testament, seen as an "ethical pattern", becomes then, as it were, a signpost. This would imply that we can in no way discard it today, and that we have to orientate ourselves accordingly in order to bring the pattern to its full realization. But if we try to absolutize the "letter" of scripture, we shall find ourselves unable to bridge the historical gap between then and now. As St. Paul says: "For the written code kills, but the Spirit gives life. . . . Now the Lord is the Spirit, and where the Spirit of the Lord is, there is freedom. And we all, with unveiled face, beholding the glory of the Lord, are being changed into his likeness from one degree of glory to another; for this comes from the Lord who is the Spirit" (2 Cor. 3, 6. 17f.). This is the paradoxical "norm" of New Testament morality.

---

without a system is based on patterns of thought. . . . The pattern touches something specific and beyond without letting it evaporate in generalities. To think philosophically is to think in patterns; the negative dialectic is a body of pattern analysis." *Idem, Eingriffe, Neun kritische Modelle* (Frankfurt a. M., 1963). One might also refer to the construction of sociological concepts in Max Weber, *Wirtschaft und Gesellschaft*. Studienausgabe (Cologne, 1964), pp. 1-42, and in general to the reaction against dominant philosophical ideas, especially in "Existentialphilosophie", where historical and sociological ideas should be more widely incorporated.

[10] Cf. L. Goppelt, "Typos," in *Theol. Wört. z N.T.* VIII, pp. 246-60.

Ildefons Lobo, O.S.B./*Prades, France*

Toward a Morality Based on the Meaning of History: The Condition and Renewal of Moral Theology

In the *Constitution on the Church in the Modern World,* the Church has for the first time put forward, as official conciliar teaching, some elements and approaches to a theology more attuned to the concrete reality of modern man. And Pope Paul VI, in his address to the Council observers in October 1963, also spoke of the need for "a concrete and historical theology".

I should like to follow the line opened up by these approaches, which the Council made its own and which have led to new and useful avenues of investigation and evangelization, and put forward a theological reflection on the moral life of the Christian— that whole complex of actions, passions, habits and relations with God and men—a reflection taking into account those factors which constitute one of the dimensions of his being and a measure of his actions: temporality and historicity. These form the framework of his earthly existence and the distinguishing condition of his human nature. At the same time, I should like to explore possible bases for an elaboration of a moral science that would take more account of the time factor as a means of access to the reality of God, our end and aim. Man can in fact fully realize himself and become capable of perfect response to the creating and redeeming Word only if he possesses a coherent view of the world and of himself through the meaning of history.

To approach any aspect of human or divine reality from the point of view of its historicity is to place oneself on an essentially existential and dynamic plane. Phenomenological observations clearly have a particular relevance in the moral field, as they give a most useful perspective concerning man and his concrete existence. This helps us understand how in effect the plan of universal salvation is worked out in the lives of men at each period of history and in different surroundings.

I

THE PLACE OF TEMPORALITY AND HISTORICITY IN THE HUMAN CONDITION

1. *Man as a Problem*

Human thought has always circled historically around three fundamental and, from the cognitive point of view, interdependent realities: God, man and the world. The extent of man's knowledge of God and the world has varied greatly over the centuries. Particularly in recent times, philosophers, theologians and scientists have progressively widened the horizons of our knowledge of the deity and our physical universe, whereas man's knowledge of himself made very little progress between classical humanism and the beginning of the 19th century. But the problem of what man is has always been a basic philosophical preoccupation.

Anthropology started by defining man in terms of mechanistic and biological causality on the basis of evolution. Interest in evolution, followed by the birth of modern technology, coincided with an awakening of man's historical sense—a prime function of the rational being. Huxley has defined man as evolution made conscious of itself.

Modern thought is clearly developing on the basis of an anthropocentric structure. Man is the first concern of the modern world and of modern thinkers. The Church is not being left out of this development and is also concentrating her attention on man and the world.[1] In the Middle Ages God was described as the sphere whose center was everywhere and whose circumference was nowhere. Later, Pascal applied this same figure of speech to the world. Today it would be transferred to man insofar as his subjectivity extends even to the realm of the transcendent. By anthropocentrism I mean here a formal mental orientation, a thought structure; in terms of the content of faith, theocentrism is required.[2]

This anthropocentrism is also apparent from the psychological angle: any conscious human affirmation of an object is an affirmation of the subject himself. And there can be no knowledge of God except through oneself, just as there can be no full knowledge of oneself without some understanding of God and of the universe that man inhabits.

2. Man's Place in the Universe

Man will only come to full realization of himself through the long and laborious mental process of assimilating the whole of creation, rationalizing it and humanizing it. The whole of creation cries out for man's intelligence to complete it through his efforts and the powers given him by God. Responsible to his creator, he is the demiurge of creation.[3] In fact, according to Genesis, man actualizes the quality of his image of God, perfects himself and fulfills his responsibilities toward his creator, precisely by constructing, dominating and presiding over the world

[1] The *Constitution on the Church in the Modern World* marks a great advance in this respect. Paul VI's closing address to Vatican Council II is also most interesting: "You modern humanists who renounce the transcendence of supreme things, at least grant it [the Council] this merit, and show yourselves capable of recognizing our new humanism: we, too, more than anyone, are devoting ourselves to man. . . . There is one more aspect we should like to emphasize: all these doctrinal riches have only one end in view: the service of man" (*Docum. Cath.* 63 [1966], n. 1462, pp. 59ff).

[2] C. Dumont, "Anthropocentrisme et formation des clercs," in *Nouv. Rev. Théol.* 87 (1965), pp. 449-65; J. B. Metz, *Christliche Anthropozentrik.* Uber den Denkform des Thomas von Aquin (Munich, 1962).

[3] M.-D. Chenu, "Corporalité et temporalité," in *L'Evangile dans le temps* (Paris, 1964), p. 432.

and other human beings (Gen. 1, 26-28). Man's insertion into the universe and solidarity with it was elaborated theologically by St. Paul, as José María González-Ruiz has shown elsewhere.[4]

This solidarity between man and the universe is worked out in the march of time. And the mere physical temporality of all matter becomes the stuff of history as soon as man's intelligence perceives the succession of events, reasons them out and gives them an explanation and a meaning. Man is the true basis of history.

3. *Temporality and Historicity*

Temporality is not a consequence of some initial failure of the human spirit. It is a result of God's plan that everything should not be made plain once and for all, but that creation should be tied to the unfolding of time in such a way that man becomes the closest collaborator in it. In this way, "God's creative undertaking gives consistence to the duration of time".[5]

What this amounts to is simply a confirmation of what the philosophers and theologians have always said—namely that time is part of the definition of man in his status of creature. As Jean Lacroix so rightly observes, Marx and Freud were quite correct in teaching that the human spirit is not only structure but also event, history.[6]

It is true that all consideration of man as an historical being and of history itself runs the risk of staying on a merely phenomenological plane, limiting itself to a sort of philosophy of evolution and merely noting historical events and the development of ideas. Any consideration of the historicity of the rational animal should have a more ambitious aim: it should endeavor to constitute an *ontology* from which human reality can be seen

[4] J. M. González-Ruiz, "Fonaments biblics per a una teologia del món," in *Qüestions de vida cristiana* 26 (1965), pp. 88-100; *idem*, "Dimensiones cósmicas de la Soteriología paulina," in *XIV Semana Bíblica Española* (Madrid, 1954), pp. 83-101.

[5] A. Hayen, "Le 'cercle' de la connaissance humaine selon St Thomas," in *Rev. Phil. de Louvain* 54 (1954), p. 589.

[6] J. Lacroix, *Marxisme, existentialisme, personnalisme. Présence de l'éternité dans le temps* (Paris, 1960).

not only through the prism of an abstract, timeless nature, but as having a nature that is essentially historical. Otherwise, our purpose of constructing a system of morality based on the meaning of history would risk falling into philosophical relativism or theological modernism. This certainly does not mean that we can neglect the discoveries of phenomenology or empirical observations concerning biological evolution, let alone the development of man's mind and the collective genius of humanity. All these are of great importance in the moral field.

Interesting studies of this matter already exist, in particular a book by J. H. van den Berg and an article by P. Antoine.[7] Van den Berg has originated a new science, which he calls "metabletics". This science, contrary to the more or less tacit suppositions of traditional psychology, affirms that certain qualitative changes have taken place in man. Comparing modern man with his forebears of a few centuries ago, he claims that certain important psychic changes can be observed. Antoine starts by denying that time is merely a commonplace of existence, neutral in respect to the events that can be dated through it, and goes on, following Bergson and Heidegger, to affirm that temporality lies at the very heart of all being. On the evidence of arithmetical and geometrical representations of the undeniable fact of the acceleration of history, he deduces important conclusions which I propose to discuss in the third part of this article.

4. *The Meaning of History*

The point of departure for an examination in depth of the meaning of history must, I think, be the idea of progress, the progress that is obvious from a comparison between the past and the present. Now it is not everywhere agreed that history has any positive meaning; today there are those who find ethical, metaphysical and scientific grounds on which to deny it.

Metaphysical grounds would be those of atheistic existential-

---

[7] J. H. van den Berg, *Metabletica ou la psychologie historique* (Paris, 1962); P. Antoine, "L'homme et le temps," in *Rev. de l'action Pop.* 178 (1964), pp. 517-36.

ism: all existence is absurd; nothing has any meaning; our sole destiny is not to have one.

Ethical grounds for denying that history has a meaning can be found in the works of Georges Bernanos and Gabriel Marcel, and also in the early Chaplin films: they all draw attention to the non-sense of history as it appears in the modern world, holding that man is dehumanizing himself through his own inventions and progress. Technical progress is even a barrier to moral and spiritual progress. History is leading mankind to collective suicide.

The scientific grounds for denial can be found in conclusions about the end of the world, such as those reached by J. Rostand, pointing to an end for humanity that is as absurd and unavoidable as the extinction of the dinosaurs: degeneration of the species, another ice age, or the earth becoming too hot for human survival.[8]

This is not the place for a critical examination of the insights— and fallacies—of these variously pessimistic denials of the meaning of history. Hegel and Marx both attempted to find a positive meaning in history, still on the purely humanist plane, through a dialectic of history confined to a reconciliation of man with himself and with nature. These philosophies divorced from transcendence seem very limited from the Christian point of view, even though Marx considered that "communism resolves the mystery of history and knows that it does so".[9]

Karl Rahner, in his conference given at the Marxist-Christian conversations in Salzburg in May, 1965, presented a profound examination of the nature and future of man, showing him as orientated toward an absolute end, the reality of God, but no less responsible in the material field on account of this. On the contrary, the fact that he is destined to an absolute end requires a compromise with the love of God that projects itself on earthly history; this love, in which man participates, should

---

[8] N. Dunas, *L'annonce de l'évangile aujourd'hui* (Paris, 1962).
[9] K. Marx, *National Ekonomie und Philosophie* (Stuttgart, 1953), p. 253.

dominate all the servitudes of nature and promote human freedom and well-being, as well as the progress of science and culture. While Christianity feels itself closely linked to earthly
history, the final end, the meaning of history, is transcendent.
To make earthly realities absolute points of reference would be
to convert human history into a utopian ideology.

5. *Historicity, Personalization and Socialization*

Modern man has a deeply-rooted conviction that the world
and humanity are on the move. Science and technology, as well
as social and religious developments, are changing the old order
of society and demanding a realistic attention to facts. They are
a clear sign that modern man needs to be in tune with the meaning of history to be conscious of his place and meaning as a
human being.

Through reflecting on himself, man has slowly come to knowledge of himself, of his personality on different levels (metaphysical, ethical, psychological, religious, spiritual) and in all
the elements (social, economic, political and historical) that
condition it. These elements are an important contribution to
man's conscious integration of his personality in the framework
of collective responsibilities. Chenu is quite right in pointing to
three main characteristics of the contemporary mind: the acquisi-
tion of a sense of history, dominion over and integration of matter, and the socialization of man on all levels.[10] This last aspect
is particularly important if we are to find a basis for the renewal
of moral theology in the meaning of history.

These three characteristics are genuine positive values con-
tributing to the development of a real sense of responsibility in
the modern Christian, which must supersede the false spirituality
that still threatens us today as it has always done. There is in
fact no opposition between what is temporal and what is spiritual
and eternal. Those Christians who hold a negative view of the

[10] M.-D. Chenu, "La pensée contemporaine pour ou contre Dieu?" in
L'Evangile dans le temps, op. cit., pp. 172-83.

temporal sphere only confirm Nietzsche's dictum that Christianity is a vulgar form of Platonism, or Marx's characterization of religious alienation as the opium of the people.

St. Thomas, some time ago, and Gilberto Porretano before him, enunciated a view of matter and temporality different from both the neo-Platonic approach and the doctrine of Augustine. Direct reading of the bible leads to a rediscovery of the historical dimensions of the plan of salvation, and the realistic philosophy of Aristotle to a recognition of the real existential depth of all creation. Thus, matter and time take on unsuspected theological significance.

Conclusion

Man reflects on himself, observes the progress of humanity, and so acquires an historical sense. And as his knowledge of himself and his significance deepens, he discovers the social dimensions of his history, which is social by definition. History neither can be nor ever has been a series of biographies, any more than human society is made up of the mere juxtaposition of laws, liberties and loves.[11] The solidarity of the human race in its historical destiny is something that stems from human nature itself; its destiny is unified by the Absolute that brought it into being, gave it the immanence in which it subsists and draws it toward transcendence through matter and time. All this constitutes the presence of the eternal in the temporal through God's intervention in history.

II

GOD'S INTERVENTION IN HISTORY: TIME AND HISTORY
AS ELEMENTS OF SALVATION

With God's intervention in history, which creates a history of collective salvation, the socialization of man acquires a saving value. This fact will illustrate what I have said about the

---

[11] M.-D. Chenu, "Corporalité et temporalité," *op. cit.*, p. 434.

meaning of history and give greater theological substance to the preceding observations. It will also show that the historical perspective is present and operative at the very heart of our religion, and so introduce new factors to be considered in trying to establish a moral theology based on the meaning of history.

1. *Sacred and Profane History*

For 2,000 years great thinkers have pondered on the incidence of sacred history in cosmic history and what some call profane history, on the possibility that the one gives meaning to the other. Eusebius of Caesarea, St. Augustine, Bossuet and Toynbee, to name but a few, have seen Christianity as the explanation and the apex of historical events. Voltaire was the first to challenge this viewpoint, with his *Essais sur les Moeurs et l'Esprit des Nations*, an attack on Bossuet's *Discours sur l'Histoire universelle*. The very fact that Bossuet began with the creation of the world and Voltaire with ancient Chinese civilization is an indication of the gulf that separates the two approaches.

Voltaire interprets history as the continuous development of civilization by which the theology of history is changed into the philosophy of history. He, in fact, was the first to use the phrase "philosophy of history" and open the way for the demythologizing of the New Testament which, particularly at the time of the *Aufklärung*, was to interpret biblical history on the principles of profane history. Voltaire, as Löwith has shown,[12] produced the theses that were later to be given a powerful theological structure by Hegel with his philosophy of the mind, and a scientific interpretation by Marx, based on the dialectic of economics.

The influences of these anti-theological currents are still with us today, although the great strides made by the theology of history have given greater substance to the true theological significance of the time factor. Marx's historical dialectic, with its—one must admit—very appealing and positive view of temporality, is still a powerful influence on contemporary

[12] K. Löwith, "L'histoire universelle et l'événement du salut," in *Dieu Viv.* 18 (1959), pp. 59-60.

thought. The historical dialectic, he claims, offers a release from every form of alienation, particularly economic and social. A great contemporary Marxist, Roger Garaudy, has written that the meaning of history is to set man free.[13] As Christians, we have no quarrel with this profound and positive vision of history, but we must add something more. For us, human failure does not lie essentially or principally in economic alienation and its consequences. We must place man's initial failure in a religious fact, the fact of sin, introducing an ontological spiritual decadence into the human field. While it is true that history is a process of liberation from servitude, it is true only insofar as God intervenes in history to give human efforts an eternal destiny. This brings us to the question of the relationship between time and eternity.

2. *Christ, the Link between Time and Eternity*

It is possible to envisage a threefold connection between cosmic time and eternity, with Christ as the link. First, there is a relationship of origin: time springs from eternity, since it takes its existence from the eternal Idea, the Word of God, always present and creating, conserving existence and prolonging the succession of ages: "All things were made through him, and without him was not anything made that was made"; "He is before all things and in him all things hold together" (Jn. 1, 3; Col. 1, 17). The second relationship deepens the connection between time and eternity, and is found in the "fullness of time": "The Word became flesh and dwelt amongst us." The incarnation is the center of cosmic history and dictates the definitive meaning of history. The third relationship is the final link, when temporality will dissolve in the eternity of God with the parousia of Christ. This, says St. Paul, will happen "when all things are subjected to him [Christ]; then the Son himself will also be subjected to him who put all things under him, that God may be everything to everyone" (1 Cor. 15, 28).

We still lack a serious exegetical work on temporality in holy

[13] R. Garaudy, *Le communisme et la morale* (Paris, 1960), p. 71.

scripture.[14] But it is not difficult to see that the whole dynamic of the bible is orientated *toward the future*. All events are orientated toward what is to come: Christ is the beginning, middle and end of history.[15]

Since the incarnation of the Word constitutes the nucleus of history and the origin of its meaning, it becomes the necessary point of reference for a discussion of the moral life of the Christian. This derives its full meaning from this event which opens the last stage of the universal historical process.

In the *Summa Theologica,* St. Thomas starts from a specifically Platonic principle of intelligibility, though shorn of the cosmic determinism this originally implied: the *exitus-reditus* concept, the concept of emanation and return. Based on this structural principle, the whole sweep of his theology opens with a sacred history: all events, man, his moral actions and habits, the world, the laws governing the universe—all take their meaning from this sacred history.

There are passages in St. Thomas that could form the basis of a theology of Christian history, above all, in his treatises on the Old Law and the New Law. The Law of the Old Testament has a slow, progressive educative function leading toward the "fullness of time". The New Law is the key to the understanding of the whole of history (Ia-IIae, 98-108).

3. *Progress as a Characteristic Element in All Human-Divine Realization*

At the beginning of the treatise on the New Law (Ia-IIae, q. 106, a. 3-4), St. Thomas asks whether it was fitting that the New Law should have been proclaimed from the beginning of history or not. His reasons in reply go beyond the mere argument from convenience that he uses. In fact, he has a very deep and realistic view of man and his temporal condition. For him, the perfection of the New Law argues that it has to be arrived

[14] Cf. P. Pidoux, "Apropos de la notion biblique du temps," in *Rev. de Theol. et Phil.* 3 (²1952), pp. 120-5; J. Barr, *Biblical Words for Time* (Naperville, 1962).

[15] Cf. J. Moroux, *Le mystère du temps* (Paris, 1962), pp. 97-8.

at gradually, since a gradual process of perfection is proper to the whole of creation, following the *rhythm of time*. This principle has important applications in moral theology. So does another historical and psychological consideration that appears elsewhere in the Summa (Ia-IIae, q. 79, a. 4): time has a particular function on the life of man and on the gradual process of his conversion to God; it gives him an experience of sin that enables him to see himself more clearly and awakens a desire and hope of improving himself through the grace of the New Covenant. God does not lead man to perfection all at once, just as he does not punish his sins on the spot. He respects his temporal condition, his slow and halting progress in his ambiguous surroundings.

The progress of the incarnation of the Word among men is also a slow one. Not without reason did the Son of God become the Word in a progressive process (Heb. 1, 1-2) before becoming flesh. So time acquires a great richness of meaning as man draws near and is converted to God, and discovers absolute reality.

4. *The Social and Material Spheres as Mediators of the History of Salvation*

We have already referred to the socializing character of the history of salvation, which is effected through a chosen people with a mission to communicate it to the rest of mankind. Christ formed a new people and a new society, the Church, of which we become members through faith in Christ in order to continue the saving work of the Messiah in time.

The incarnation of the Word also produces a change in the communication of salvation and in the process of divinization. When Christ came among men in human flesh, the eternal took deeper root in the temporal sphere. From this moment on, and more particularly after Pentecost, salvation history was not communicated by the direct and transcendental intervention of God in human affairs, as in the history of the Old Covenant, but generally through secondary causes. Words, gestures and materials are taken up in the sacraments as signs that communicate a divine and transcendent reality. Newman, in his *Apologia,* put forward a threefold principle which corresponds to this: the *hierarchical* principle (the human mediation of authority as service); the *dogmatic* principle (the mediation of scripture and the *"sensus Ecclesiae"* in the knowledge of God); and the *sacramental* principle (the mediation of word and matter in the communication of salvation).

Conclusion

With the incarnation of Christ, temporal and eternal, material and spiritual are more deeply united, and history receives the fullness of its meaning. Christianity is an historical religion, working itself out in close union with the passing of time. The parables compare the kingdom of God to the mustard seed, the smallest of all seeds, which grows into the greatest of shrubs; to the leaven which leavens the whole meal; to the wheat among which the weeds are left until both are grown; to servants waiting for their master to come home from the marriage feast—all these are images that emphasize the time factor and the value of progress in relation to the sphere of the transcendent and eternal. Temporal realities, furthermore, are seen not as obstacles but as potentialities.

If these lessons are applied to Christian morality, certain conclusions emerge.

III

CHRISTIAN MORALITY, CONSCIOUS OF THE TIME FACTOR AND THE DYNAMISM OF HISTORY

It is not easy to summarize all that the moral theologian can deduce from philosophical and theological reflections on temporality and history in a few pages. But there are certain aspects whose application in the field of moral theology seems to have been somewhat overlooked. A moral theology based on the meaning of history must, it seems to me, take account of an initial postulate and certain determining factors.

1. *The Historical Catholicity of Our Religion*

Catholicity should not be confined to the geographical factor, but must also be understood in relation to time. Just as each race or country brings its own values to Christianity and lives its Christianity in its own particular form, so each age or civilization brings its own style, peculiarities and differing emphases to the way in which the permanent realities of the Gospel are lived.

Theology, as much as the natural sciences, is limited and is to a certain extent provisional by its very nature. St. Thomas taught that theology is subordinate to the science of God and the saints in heaven, the science that is complete and unchangeable; our science is consequently always limited and subject to a process of unending development, not static but dynamic, not definite but provisional, just as Christ said to his apostles that there were many things that they could not bear at the time, but which would gradually be revealed to them (Jn. 16, 12-13).

Pius XII stated in 1949: "The mystical body of Christ, like the physical members of which it is made up, does not live and move in the abstract, outside the constantly variable conditions of time and space. It is not and cannot be separated from the world that surrounds it; it is always of its time; it progresses with its time, day by day, hour by hour, continually adapting its manners and attitudes to those of the society in whose midst it must function." [16] Absolute fidelity to the Gospel of Christ in fact requires this agility in adaptation proposed by Pius XII.

Moral theologians must make the effort to recognize the "signs of the times" to which John XXIII alluded in *Pacem in terris* and, more explicitly, in his opening speech to Vatican Council II. It is not without reason that the *Constitution on the Church in the Modern World* emphasized the profound changes taking

---

[16] Pius XII, Address to the staff and students of the Seminary of Anagni, April 20, 1949.

place in the world around us and in the human condition in a technical and urban civilization. But it is also true that the Council did not undertake a fundamental revision of moral theology. The conciliar documents, in particular the *Constitution on the Church in the Modern World,* do however contain, or at least suggest, certain postulates that moral theologians should continue to investigate. In so doing, they must take account of new developments in anthropology, sociological observations, and the positive value of historical events which the early Christian writers rightly called *praeparatio evangelica.* The Church is in fact now leading us officially toward that "concrete and historical theology" to which Pope Paul VI referred, which opens up new perspectives in the field of moral theology.

It is not, therefore, either surprising or alarming if Christian morality, while retaining its original essential characteristics, has in the 20th century different views on politics, war, society, worldly goods, money, sexual pleasure, etc., to those held in the 4th, 9th or 14th centuries. This is not bringing dangerous relativism into morality, but applying the principle of the historical catholicity of our religion, a principle that stems from the very natural law of the evolutionary process ordained by God.

2. *A Moral Theology of Progress*

Progress is an observable fact at all levels of existence. It guarantees the meaning of history. God has created nothing static. The whole cosmos is subject to the process of time, the motor of progress. God has given his creatures and the whole universe temporality so that they can realize and develop themselves in a gradual progress toward the end he has assigned to them. One of the properties of time is to be a connotation of the creative activity of God.[17]

Man, too, sustained and empowered by grace, must by his efforts advance "from one degree of glory to another" (2 Cor. 3, 18). The Christian moral code, which orders and directs this

[17] C. Tresmontant, *Essais sur la pensée hébraïque* (Paris, 1965), p. 26.

process of development, cannot go on appearing to operate by subjecting man to an abstract law or a set of "rules of the game" by which he will "be saved", and which will tell him whether he is sinning or not. Christian virtue consists in the *progressive* awakening of the divine spark that is present in each one of us, until God is "everything to everyone". In his magnificent treatise on the New Law (Ia-IIae, q. 106), St. Thomas taught that it consists not so much in the written law as in the grace of the Holy Spirit, which is, of course, far more demanding than observance of the letter of the law. The process is a sort of symbiosis with divinity.

Being a Christian is not like being English or American, or tall or short. It is a reality that is never fully realized. As Kierkegaard said: "One never *is* a Christian in the full sense of the word, but one goes on becoming or making oneself a Christian." The New Testament lays frequent stress on this process of *transformation* into a divine being. Remember the parables that express the idea of this progress and growth. Thus it is not surprising that one of the severest phrases that scripture puts into the mouth of the Lord is aimed at those who settle for mediocrity: "Would that you were cold or hot! So, because you are lukewarm, and neither cold nor hot, I will spew you out of my mouth" (Apoc. 3, 15-16).

Sin should be seen in the context of this dynamism of the kingdom of God. Sin is to make a means an end. It is a refusal to see people, things or events in relation to what is to come, the reality of God. Sin kills the progress of the spirit and negates the meaning of history.

From the foregoing it should be clear that Christian morality should lay great stress on *hope,* and the essence of hope is a positive approach to time.[18] Hope is based on the sureness of progress and the certainty that absolute reality, the Absolute toward whom we make progress, is slowly revealing himself. Hope, Gabriel Marcel has said, is the virtue of open time and is

---

[18] J. Daniélou, *Evangile et monde moderne* (Tournai, 1960), p. 102.

essentially prophetic.[19] From this it follows that the Christian's being is not limited to what he is *now,* but embraces what he must be and will be when time is absorbed into eternity.

Moral catechesis should show Christian life as a process of self-realization and growth toward the kingdom of God in accordance with the meaning of the history of salvation, which impinges on universal history. It is a process of progress based on the hope that God will become everything to everyone. A moral catechesis like this, vitalized by sacramental theology, cannot fail to give a tremendous impetus to our Christian life, particularly as man is today very conscious of the meaning of such concepts as progress, the dynamic of history, self-fulfillment, etc.

A practical result of this will be that this morality of progress will avoid evaluating the Christian according to his moral standing at a given moment—sinning or not sinning much, observing all the commandments or not (morality of sin and legalistic morality), and will judge him according to his *basic approach* to God's call. The sinner constantly falling back into sin but genuinely struggling to make progress cannot be considered worse than the Christian who leads a mediocre life without having to accuse himself of grave sins, but whose Christianity is static and fails to take advantage of the time God gives him for the maturation and development of his personality.

I believe that a definition of morality must emphasize the dynamism inherent in it and basic to it. That given by Sertillanges: "Morality is the science of what man *should be* in function of what he *is*", seems good in this respect. Man is never yet fully himself, and will not be until he knows fully who he is, what his properties are, what he is to become, where he comes from and where he is going, why he lives in time and why he must enter into eternity, and so on. These are the basic questions of all human existence, questions that are now asked with more

[19] G. Marcel, "Structure de l'espérance," in *Dieu Viv.* 19 (1951), pp. 75-7.

urgency than ever before. A moral theology based on the meaning of history must try to give the answers to them.

3. *Morality and Personal Development*

The aim of Christian morality is the divinization of man by
Christ, the sacrament of our encounter with God.[20] This is to be
achieved by making maximum use of man's human qualities so
that he fulfills his temporal responsibilities to the full.

Man's voyage of self-discovery in recent times has been
helped by philosophical and theological investigations into history which have produced an anthropocentric view of the cosmos
not necessarily involving a rejection of God. There can be no
competition between creature and creator. God's greatness and
transcendence can be safeguarded without belittling man and
the whole of creation. Once the idea of God as an infinite being,
creator and redeemer, is accepted, everything else inevitably
depends absolutely on him. God and what is not God cannot be
added and subtracted. The more we affirm the greatness of man
as the king of creation and a being divinized by the sacrifice of
Christ—without forgetting his defects and weaknesses—the more
we emphasize the greatness and wisdom of God who has pre-
ordained a cosmos presided over by a being capable of observing his own progress toward God and of giving it a meaning.

The Christian view of the meaning of history is bound to lay
particular stress on the personal development of man, if it is to
attain to a clear view of man's mission in the cosmos, a mission
that is a transcendent one by virtue of the fact that man is a
spiritual being.

A truly contemporary moral theology must stress these aspects
of human personality and encourage man to fulfill his temporal
responsibilities. There is much to be learned here from exegesis
based on the theology of St. Paul, and much that moral theology
has to teach about the nature of the "Christian being".

---

[20] E. Schillebeeckx, *Christ, the Sacrament of the Encounter with God*
(London & New York, 1965).

4. *Morality and Socialization*

The word "socialization" is here used in a broad sense to designate the interdependence of different human groups and the fact that all men participate in the same collective responsibilities, phenomena that are becoming more and more marked with the progress of history. Christian morality cannot rest content with merely registering the fact of these phenomena. It must aid their development to the maximum and recognize that they play their part in the unfolding of the plan of salvation.

The phenomena that make up the process of socialization in the modern world correspond admirably, it is interesting to note, with the basic demands of Christian revelation governing human relations—total openness and generosity toward one's neighbor, expressed in terms of love and charity. These requirements also coincide with the findings of modern psychology, which insist on the need for interpersonal relations for the development of a mature personality. The process is therefore one of the constituents of the meaning of history.

In this situation, Christian morality cannot just fall back on repetition of the Scholastic theses on love of one's neighbor and their subsequent casuistic elaborations. Human relationships today present completely new problems because they involve a completely new set of social relationships on the psychological, economic, cultural and religious levels.

One fact that is certain is that as history progresses, Christendom is disappearing. The Church is losing her privileged and predominant position in the arts, social culture, politics and other fields. The Church seems to be ridding herself of the worldly clericalism of the past so as to become no more than the ferment of divine life that leavens the whole meal, as indeed Christ described it and wished it (Mt. 13, 33). The disciples of Christ have become—if they have not in fact always been—a *pusillus grex*.

This in no way justifies the maintenance of certain forms of moral education and catechesis aimed at sheltering Christians in a closed ghetto of otherworldly spirituality, a ghetto whose rarified atmosphere will be a "refuge" and "protection" from the pagan world that is destined for perdition. Christian existence, lived in the history of salvation, is, as we have seen, closely linked to the destiny of humanity and cannot be dissociated from what some would call the profane content of human life. Ordinary mundane tasks and the collective responsibility to build a new and better world are just as much incumbent on the Christian as on the atheist, if not more so, though the meaning each attributes to them will no doubt be somewhat different.

Unfortunately our moral theology still remains strongly centered on a morality of the individual, and of the individual act divorced from the totality of Christian life. Collective sin is a concept that most Christians have not yet grasped. We should instead be insisting on social responsibilities in the fields of politics, culture and group relations. These are the real responsibilities of Christians in a socialized world; this is also the area in which the performance of Christianity will be judged in comparison with that of an atheistic humanism whose sensitivity to collective responsibilities is very highly developed. One has only to think of such writers and thinkers as Marx, Malraux, Camus and Sartre to see this.

5. *The Virtuous Life*

Finally, I should like to examine what a consideration of the time factor can mean for the practice of the virtues in man's life. We have seen that temporality makes progress possible, but it must be added that temporality conditions progress today in a manner very different from that of past centuries.

As P. Antoine has shown by relating the constant of time graphically to progress and evolution, history is undergoing an extraordinary process of acceleration, in the sense that while centuries ago progress in a given period of time was minimal, today not only progress but the acceleration of progress in the same period of time is enormous. These are simply empirical observations of a fact with important consequences in the moral formation of man today, consequences that cannot be ignored in either education or moral theology.

Man today is overwhelmed by the pressure of events and the rapidity of evolution and progress. He has no time to reflect on events and convert them into effective experience. And experience itself has less value than it had previously, since the grounds of reality are constantly shifting and situations are always new. Solutions foreseen and formulas based on type turn out to be inadequate. The life of virtue which the young used to learn from their elders should still be shown to them as an example, but the young today cannot take their standards *only* from the customs, manners and behavior of their elders.

The same process can be seen at work in the field of professional formation. The technician and scientist have to be informing themselves constantly if they are not to fall behind in their professional knowledge. The old person who finds himself caught up in this whirlwind of change can easily tire of trying to keep up, cling tenaciously to his own experience and the tradition he has inherited and look nostalgically back to the securities of the past. The young on the other hand find that the past cannot offer them sufficient guidance for the present, and that a surer source of guidance is to look toward the future. A concrete example of the working of this progress in the moral field could be the virtue of prudence.

Prudence occupied a prominent position in Aristotle's system of ethics, and was taken over by St. Thomas into his theological synthesis. Aristotelian prudence is in fact the virtue of judging action on the basis of experience. Antoine, in a telling graph, shows how, with the acceleration of history, retrospective prudence is no longer sufficient. Not only is it possible for the present situation to have no precedents that can have been registered by experience, but it is certain that the future will contain a number of elements that cannot be foreseen now. Therefore, for prudence to be really prudent today, it must become a firmly *prospective* virtue. And Aristotelian prudence must of course be complemented by a theology of Christian time, of the *kairos* as an *absolutely original* moment in which God is revealing himself to man and arousing an adequate and generous response in him through his grace.

Aristotle's whole ethical scheme needs to be considered in the light of modern anthropology and the attitudes that an industrial and urban civilization require of the Christian.

There is another aspect of the temporal process that leads to a criticism of casuistic morality. Some time ago, economists observed that some processes worked themselves out in long cycles and some in short cycles. Jacques Leclercq has applied these short-term and long-term laws to the sphere of human conduct.[21] Thus, for example, casuistic morality is a system for judging the short term; it is very much concerned with individual acts and very little with the building up of the future. It mistrusts time and concentrates on the immediate present.

A doctrinally sound catechesis which insisted on the *basic attitudes* of the person and a morality of virtues rather than actions, on the other hand, would lead to a long-term moral theology. Its fruits would, no doubt, take longer to appear, but when they did, they would be more mature and longer lasting. Morality should in fact form consciences in such a way that obligations would be fulfilled not because of precept or the imposition of a law, but because the desire to fulfill them sprang from the deep inner dispositions of the Christian being. In education, for example, rules should never be laid down without a convincing explanation of the need for them, so that the child would observe them from the promptings of his own conscience, helped, of course, by an indication of what the rules are.

Fidelity to the basic requirements of the Gospel must become deep conviction, and this conviction must be closely tied to our temporality, so that it remains alive and operative through the whole of man's time span and the crises it brings—physiological crises such as puberty, middle age, illnesses, old age; sociological crises such as examinations, change of surroundings, work, economic difficulties; interpersonal crises such as friendship, love,

---

[21] J. Leclercq, *Penser chrétiennement notre temps* (Paris, 1951).

marriage, infidelities, deaths, etc. Grace does not free us from these vicissitudes of time, but it does enable us to recognize their saving value if we know how to read the "signs of the times" and possess the certainty that "in everything God works for good with those who love him".

IV

CONCLUSION

To be of our time, moral theology, more than any other theological discipline, must take account of the extremely fruitful findings of the empirical sciences, of anthropology and the philosophy and theology of history, if it is to produce valid new syntheses.

There is a general movement of return to sources, and to this moral theology should add a new degree of "incarnation" in the world, abandoning the ivory tower of timelessness in which it has taken refuge. Matter, man, historical events, the "signs of the times" in general, are the new *loci theologici*. They are the setting for the encounter between God and man. When man finds his very temporality—wisely accepted, analyzed and used without falling into a sterile, narcissistic rejection of the transcendent—a richness of grace, then this temporality will become the source of a greater degree of reality and dynamism in the moral life of the Christian. The *Pastoral Constitution on the Church in the Modern World* represents a real advance in this respect in the official teaching of the Church on man and temporal realities in general. Man, in fact, possesses a divine spark that impels him toward eternity. In him, time and eternity meet.

Peter Benenson/*London, England*

The Natural Law and Statute Law: A Lawyer's View

The production of laws is one of the busiest industries of the 1960's. Parliaments work late into the night; even so they cannot complete the enormous volume of legislative business that the government demands. To cope with the shortage of parliamentary time, it is becoming common practice for the legislature to delegate powers of law-making to government departments. And the departments are not always able to keep up with the pace so that there is now a spate of what lawyers call sub-delegated legislation, that is, regulations issued by some board established upon the authority of a government department. The vast mass of law pouring off the presses of the government printer is more than any single lawyer can assimilate; he is forced to rely on abstracts and indexes to chart his passage through the sea of new legislation. The man in the street is completely lost.

I

STATUTE LAW IN A TECHNOLOGICAL SOCIETY

The whole of this outpouring of law can conveniently be called statute law. It differs from the common law in that it is not in any sense a codification of the attitudes and traditions of the people. It is designed to meet the changing conditions of technological society; it is imposed from above; it does not spring up from below. Statute law is equally distinct from natural law in that it is very much a feature of the fragmentation of the world into mutually exclusive sovereign States. It depends for its enforcement upon the authority of the State, not upon the good sense of the human race.

Parallel with this increase in law-making is a disturbing rise in the number of people employed to enforce the law. These are by no means just police, but include civil servants whose duty it is to inspect, verify, examine, check and report. All of them are subtracted from the total number of men and women available to produce food, minerals or manufactures. The cost of paying them and accommodating them in new buildings is a cause of steadily rising taxation, which many qualified observers believe to be a major cause of law-breaking.

It was a leading British socialist lawyer—a present minister—who said that he thought that as soon as the general level of taxation exceeded 40%, the law of declining returns entered into force. Whether he was right about the exact level is a matter for varying opinion, but there is little doubt that there comes a point in the scale of taxation when even the most law-abiding sections of the community start to evade their liability. Once this stage has been reached, it becomes progressively more difficult to enforce non-fiscal laws, for those sections of the community which lack any strong tradition of their own are naturally drawn to follow the example set by the wealthiest. It is fashionable today to blame the young for lawlessness, but the absence of any sense of obligation to carry out the spirit of the law is something which they have learned from a senior generation of tax-evaders.

To quote another distinguished contemporary Briton—this time a leading judge, Lord Denning, people "obey the law because they know that it is a thing they *ought* to do". This statement reflects the thinking of the period when the judge was a young man. It is questionable whether contemporary youth would express their attitude to law in quite the same way. Many would say that the principal reason why they obeyed the law was a fear of detection. The enormous volume of law-making has inevitably depreciated the value of and respect for the laws. It is one thing to accept with heart and mind the Mosaic law that "thou shalt not steal"; it is another to obey instantaneously a regulation which requires vehicles weighing more than 3 tons to be parked on alternate sides of the street on odd and even days of the week between 9 A.M. and 6 P.M.

It is this writer's submission that unless legislatures accept certain principles of law-making, our highly industrialized societies will degenerate into anarchy, due to declining respect for the law accelerated by higher taxation imposed to pay for law-enforcement made necessary because people less and less think that they *ought* to obey the law—a truly vicious circle. Stated in a positive form, this proposition reads: Laws in order to command respect must coincide with the general will of the people. This proposition is taken from the classical theory of natural law as developed during the latter half of the 18th century.

II

EIGHT PRINCIPLES OF LAW-MAKING IN INDUSTRIAL SOCIETIES

Jurists have rightly been suspicious of the term "the general will". It is not a precise term, but it is the most convenient way of expressing the overwhelming desire of mankind to cooperate in the creation of a harmonious community. It is the mean average of community spirit. Laws which do not appeal to that spirit are bad laws, and like all bad laws they will end by destroying the community which their makers wished to protect.

The mean average of community spirit varies throughout history and geography. The principles of law-making which are here considered are those which apply to the type of society which exists in Western Europe, North America and Australasia in the 1960's. They are not immutable principles. As the poet Tennyson says: "The old order changeth, yielding place to new, and God fulfills himself in many ways, lest one good custom should corrupt the world."

1. *Equality of Application*

The first of the eight principles is that the law should apply equally to every citizen. Few would quarrel with this principle and most legislators would say that it is axiomatic. Yet there has grown up an exempt class of citizens in contemporary societies. To quote one example which was so frequently brought up in Britain in the autumn of 1966: while all private industries and services have been compelled to freeze their charges, the post office has just increased the price of stamps and telephone calls. Another more general example of exclusion is the exception which permits the executive to open private letters and monitor telephone conversations. Clearly, powers given to the police to intercept communications increase the likelihood of crime detection, but few legislators realize that, by countenancing laws which create excluded classes in society, they are making an atmosphere in which more crime is committed.

2. *Comprehensibility*

The second principle is that law should be ascertainable and certain. Again there is general lip-service to this assertion, but that is all. An ever greater part of the legislation relating to the economic activity of society is only just comprehensible after the most careful study, and if England is a fair sample, some is complete gibberish. Granted that it is sometimes difficult to translate involved economic concepts into ordinary language, only too often little attempt is made. The laws are drawn up in a government office by a parliamentary draftsman who over the years has developed an esoteric jargon; no effort is made to recruit prose writers to the machinery of legislation. And such is the pressure of time on the legislature that back-bench members of parliament have neither opportunity nor facility to submit written amendments expressed in clearer language. The jargon-law goes on its way through parliament, often understood by no one, not even the minister who introduces it or the opposition spokesman who calls for its rejection, both of whom rely upon a brief prepared by some specialist in their entourage. There has been a resounding debate throughout the world about the degree of ownership of or control over production which should be exercised by the State. Yet rarely asserted is the simple proposition that if a law affecting economic activity cannot be made in reasonably comprehensive language, it should not be made at all. But there it is; there are situations which cannot be dealt with by law, some because they are too intimate and personal, others because they are too complicated and impersonal.

3. *Let the People Talk Before a Law Is Passed*

According to the third principle, people need to know that before a law is introduced which adversely affects their interests, they have had an adequate opportunity to make representations. Citizens of the 1960's not only realize that it is impracticable for them to take part in the process of law-making, but they actually prefer to escape from most opportunities that are given to them. The low attendance at meetings and elections of such voluntary organizations as trade unions and cooperative societies shows that the citizen of today prefers to hand over administration to the specialist. As a leisure pursuit the transaction of public business ranks poorly. People today are content to let the lawmaker get about his business, provided that they have a right to object when a law is projected which may hurt their business. The old tag, *vox populi suprema lex* (the will of the people is the supreme law), should be rephrased to read *ante legem clamor populi* (let the people talk before a law is passed). Expressed in this way it applies as much to authoritarian States as well as to democracies. Indeed, it could be argued that the communist and corporate State are both attempts to put this principle into practice by institutionalizing workers who have the same economic interest. If people are led to believe that they are denied any hope of ever altering a law, then they will turn to belief in the violent overthrow of the law, which is what is now happening in South Africa. White South Africans have failed to appreciate that it is feasible and in their own interest to consult the wishes of black Africans without necessarily involving themselves in a parliament with a large majority of black members. Man in contemporary society is an economic force, not a color symbol.

4. *Reasonableness*

The next requirement is that the law should be reasonable. In a progressively more educated society individuals are no longer prepared to accept laws because they are made by people with a higher education than their own; they need to be satisfied that the law accords with their own reason. An example of this is to be found in the differing degrees of obedience to traffic lights on the one hand and speed limits on the other. Any thinking person can see for himself that at a crossroad one stream of traffic or the other must have priority. It is less obvious that the ideal maximum speed in built-up areas is 50 miles an hour; some people argue that there is as much danger in driving too slowly as in driving too fast, and that the real vice both in town and country is in overtaking. Much modern legislation does deal with transportation; the great bulk of it appeals to the man in the street because he realizes that unless there is regulation of movement, he will never be able to arrive anywhere. But where some new regulation is introduced which does not immediately strike the mind as reasonable, as does a green and red traffic light, he needs to be assured that the regulation has been tried out experimentally and has produced benefits. Legislation after experimentation is an important development in technological societies. One point needs to be stressed. Men will only accept the results of the trials provided they know that they have a free press. Reports of results published in a government controlled or influenced newspaper deceive few readers.

5. Not Offensive to Habit

Another principle of obedience is that the law should not run contrary to habit. This is surely the correct statement of the interrelation between law and morality. Insofar as morality accords with reason, those laws which have a moral content will tend to command obedience. But the morality of a society does not always accord with reason; it depends very largely on what is taught in the nursery. Morality is officially Christian in many countries where practicing church-goers are fewer than the number of shopkeepers. Parents go on instructing their children in Christian morals—and expecting the schools to do the same—although they have long since ceased to practice these morals themselves. This is because all of us, as we grow older, look back with increasing affection on our childhood, and we are so attached to our youthful memories that we instinctively seek to impose them on the next generation. Thus morality changes very much more slowly than the rest of society. But change it does. In the State of New York it is still nominally a criminal offense to commit adultery, yet adulterous association has become so commonly accepted that if the police were to seek to apply the law, there would be general commotion. In that field of personal behavior covered by nursery and schoolroom instruction, the legislature must be careful not to run far in advance of prevailing habit.

6. Enforceability

The sixth requirement is that the law should be enforceable. This is to say that it should be enforceable without a cost and effort incommensurate with the object. For instance, many visitors to Britain are shocked by the number of licensed betting establishments. Certainly they represent a side of British life which is depressing and tawdry. But there is little merit in the accusation that the government which first permitted betting shops "legalized betting". The fact of the matter is that there was already so much street-corner betting that it was impossible to suppress it and ridiculous to try. Faced with such a situation, it is better for a government to reduce gambling by the imposition of taxes, which seem to all to be reasonable, than by the weak arm of the law. For unless people see that the law truly has a strong and effective arm, not only will that law fall into contempt, but so will all the others. Turning for a moment back to the subject of fiscal laws, if efforts are made to adhere too rigidly to the principle of the last penny, the tax-collection law may turn out not to be a collecting bowl but a vegetable strainer. If the time taken to identify the law-breaker is so long that he can whistle while he waits, the law will soon become unenforceable. It is much better to have a rough-and-ready system of tax collection which works quickly than a delicately constructed piece of machinery which moves at the pace of a tortoise. To be acceptable to the general will, a law must be enforceable with both economy and expedition.

7. *The Law Should Not Be Retroactive*

The principle that a law should not be retroactive is widely recognized. The basis for this is that the law at any time must be sure and hard. If people think that there is any likelihood that the government will suddenly legislate to require their bank to pay over their assets, they will cease to deposit money at their bank. Similarly, if they fear that some activity which is legal today will tomorrow retrospectively be declared illegal, they will not know where they are, and they will retire either into inactivity or secrecy. The principle against retroactivity needs to be widened to accord with the general will; truly stated, it should read: there must be adequate notice of any impending change in the law. Hurried laws are likely to be bad laws; hurry in enforcement only produces a fluster of evasion. People must be given sufficient time to comply with changes in the law at their pace; not every business has a full-time legal advisor at hand.

8. *Availability*

Lastly, the law must be easily available. This means that it must be accessible without extravagant cost in time or money. It is not just a question of making sure that a copy of each law is somewhere to be found in the town hall or public library; it must be available to be taken away and read. More than that, it must be issued in such a way that it can be conveniently stored and traced by a running index. According to lawyers, *ignorantia legis haud excusat* (ignorance of the law is no excuse), but the maxim is meaningless except on the basis that each person has the law drawn to his attention by the legislator. It is arguable whether or not printed copies of legislation should be made available free of charge to the citizen by right or by convenience. Strictly speaking, every member of a club should be entitled to a free copy of its regulations in return for his subscription. Should not the citizen who pays taxation at least be entitled to the rules of the State without extra charge? On the other hand, people notoriously pay scant attention to that for which they do not have to pay. The right compromise might be for the text of all laws to be available free of cost and supplied automatically to those thought likely to be affected, but that a charge should be made for the virtually indispensable binder and index.

Here, then, are eight guiding principles to encourage respect for the law: equality of application, comprehensibility, prior consultation with adverse interests, reasonableness, not offensive to habit, enforceability, adequate notice and easy availability. If they were all observed, there would be less statute law than there is today. But is that necessarily a bad thing? We are all agreed that the regulation of traffic is in the interest of the community at large and the individual in particular. But if differing traffic signs are erected every few paces along the road, however sensible each of their injunctions may be, their combined effect will be one of total confusion. There can be too many laws in a community; human beings are still creatures of instinct and impulse. If they cannot blow their nose or walk on a piece of grass without thinking first whether they are breaking a law, they will develop ugly frustrations.

III

NATURAL LAW AND STATUTE LAW

It has been said earlier that these principles relating to statute law flow from a doctrine of natural law. Is there a separate system of natural law which may conflict with and sometimes override State law? There have been many distinguished theologians and jurists who have written long books about the natural law. It is with diffidence that in a very short compass this much less learned writer puts forward a contemporary and practical viewpoint.

God created the universe of which man is part. The creation of the universe represents the process of bringing order out of chaos. Man is the highest form of life on this earth because he is the force most capable of producing a harmonious order that will preserve the existence of his own and all other species. Man's striving toward harmony on earth is thus an expression of God's will. Man's method of promoting harmony is by the creation of ever greater communities. Thus, man's desire to become part of a community is similarly an expression of God's will. The extent to which each individual desires to belong to a wider community varies with himself, his time and his place. The mean average desire to belong to a particular State, sometimes called the general will, must be respected by the legislators of that State; otherwise the desire to belong will wither and fail—and the State itself, too, in the end.

Continuing this progression of thought, man is ever reaching out for a wider range of harmony. *Non progredi regredi est* (not to go forward is to retreat). This search for a wider harmony involves the merging of the functions of one community into another greater community. The moon is shortly to be brought within the ambit of man's government. Earthbound communities will have to adjust themselves to this change of horizon; those communities which cannot adjust will atrophy, for the virility of any society is to be judged by its capacity to adapt itself to technological improvement. This is not only the law of the dinosaur, but also the law of God.

At the present time, in the 1960's, there is a growing body of dedicated men and women seeking to create a single world community. Already they are working to give effect to the various international conventions and to the Universal Declaration of Human Rights, which are the rudiments of international statute law. In seeking to justify their preference for international over national statute, some of these reformers refer to their version of natural law. They claim that there are certain divinely-inspired ordinances of an immutable character which have precedence over all other types of legislation. An example they quote is the Mosaic law that "thou shalt not kill". One purpose of the creation of a world community would be to exclude inter-State wars and to prevent people from being needlessly killed. It is submitted here that this is an erroneous concept of natural law, in which there is to be found no absolute prohibition against killing. Indeed, animals and plants have to be killed to provide food. The true concept of natural law is that in inherent compliance with his predestined function to create order out of chaos man seeks to create ever-widening communities. From this it follows that anything which is conducive to the stability and ultimate growth of a community until it encompasses the whole earth is in accordance with natural law. Further, nothing is more vital for a community than a generally accepted system of statutes —of such is made its backbone—whether the community is a small village or the entire earth. Those principles which lead to the general and willing acceptance of statutes are therefore an important part of natural law, and it is about *them* that this essay has been written.

Heinz-Horst Schrey/*Heidelberg, W. Germany*

Beyond Natural Law and Positivism

Foundations of Law in Present-
Day Evangelical Theology in
the German-Speaking World

I

The Historical Starting Point

At the turn of the century there were two particular landmarks
that were distinctive of the theological ethics of Protestantism. On
the one hand, deriving from Kant, there was the stress placed
upon the disposition and upon moral autonomy, and the emphasis
upon the free inner assent to the good by the moral subject,
leading to the laying down of material norms in the separate departments of morality where the individual was thought of as his
own lawgiver. In addition, there was the ascendency of the historical outlook and the romantic inheritance, the prominence
given to the individual and the historically unique, introducing
irrationalism. This made theology allergic to any suspicions of a
morality that moved in the realm of generalizations, universal
concepts and the truths of abstract reason. Some confusion arose
through the naive equation of the general cultural progress with
the advance of the kingdom of God and its realization in the life
of the world.

The long tradition of the unity of throne and altar, along
with the alliance between theology and German idealism, had
built up a large reserve of confidence, especially in the sphere
of political ethics. It was held that the State could not be anything but the visible embodiment of morality, and that the legal

norms it laid down could not but be in harmony with the moral code. Starting from these assumptions, it was relatively easy to come to terms with the legal positivism which sees law as the ordinance of the State and the product of its power. If the political norms showed any deviations from individual morality, recourse was sought in an irrational reference to the hidden workings of God who, even as he slays, brings to life again, and whose love can assume stern and even apparently paradoxical forms. Men were not prepared to see that in the political growths of imperialism and colonialism or in the developments of capitalism a breach had been made with the principles underlying the traditional norms of Christian civilization. Two particular events were necessary before their eyes could be opened. On the one hand, there was the worldwide disruption caused by two world wars and the experience of totalitarian dictators; on the other, there was a new theological revolution that rose above the subjectivism and irrationalism handed down by tradition.[1]

In what follows, an attempt will be made to give some account of the new start for ethics that resulted from the renaissance under Luther and the rediscovery of the bible, with special attention to the ethics of law.

II

THE ORIGINS OF AN EVANGELICAL ETHICS OF LAW

The politicizing and ideologizing of law in the Third Reich had served to demonstrate the limits of a pure legal positivism and led to an urgent quest for a transpositive system of law. After the year 1945, both the administration of the law[2] and the philos-

---

[1] As early as 1918, it was quite clear in ecclesiastical circles that World War I had brought the world to a "critical turning point". Cf. K.-W. Dahm, *Pfarrer und Politik* (Cologne-Opladen, 1965: Dortmunder Schriften zur Sozialforschung, 29). For an attempt to show the progress of irrationalism in philosophy from Nietzsche up to the Fascist regimes, see particularly G. Lukács, *Die Zerstörung der Vernunft* (Neuwied and Berlin, 1962).

[2] The Constitutional Court of the Bundesrepublik proclaimed as one of its first decisions that it "recognized the existence of suprapositive law

ophy of jurisprudence[3] were based upon a transpositive law by which lawmaking was to be measured and judged. As possible metaphysical foundations, both the Catholic doctrine of natural law and the modern value-philosophy of M. Scheler and N. Hartmann both lay ready at hand. But Evangelical philosophy also felt called to make its contribution at this point. The common starting point that had been accepted in the ecumenical field was the revealed will of God; it alone could be the Christian's binding authority. And so, at the International Study-Group of the World Council of Churches held at Wadham College in 1949, certain guidelines for the interpretation of holy scripture were laid down, expressing the common convictions of all the members of the World Council of Churches who were at that meeting.

But how do men experience this will of God? There was general agreement among all the Christian bodies that this comes about in some way or other through revelation. To be sure, there were notable differences of opinion when it came to laying down the manner in which the revealed will of God applies to the sphere of law. At Wadham College, it was only possible to aim at agreement on the basis that "no teaching that is in clear contradiction to the bible standpoint can be considered Christian", but it was not possible to reach agreement on the questions of the authority of tradition, reason and natural law. Thus there has been "a renewal—in more intense form—of the old and difficult problem as to whether man has to rely exclusively on divine revelation in holy scripture to find out the will of God, or whether he can advance at least some part of the way along another road by the use of his reasoning powers which enable him to recognize the works of God in nature and history".[4]

---

that is binding even for the constitution-maker, and that it is requisite . . . to measure the established law by its standards" (*Juristenzeitung*, 1951, p. 729).

[3] Cf. G. Radbruch, "Gesetzliches Unrecht und übergesetzliches Recht," in *Rechtsphilosophie* (Stuttgart, ⁴1950, pp. 347ff.; H. Coing *Rechtsphilosophie* (Berlin, 1950).

[4] The quotation is from H. Simon, *Der Rechtsgedanke in der gegenwärtigen deutschen evangelischen Theologie unter besonderer Berücksichtigung des Problems materialer Rechtsgrundsätze*. A dissertation before the Faculty of Legal Science at the University of Bonn, 1952, p. 49.

Thus there would seem to be four different lines of approach to the theological basis of law, in accordance with the dogma of the Trinity: (1) Law is based upon the government of God the creator and the creative ordinances of the world that he has made. (2) Law must be understood as the expression of God as sustainer, whose ordinances are there to sustain his creation in a world of fallen beings. (3) Law can be linked up with the central saving act of God the reconciler and the appearance of the divine righteousness in Jesus Christ. (4) A fourth possibility is provided by a different view, which would seek to combine the three theological foundations set out above in a salvational and trinitarian synthesis. No attempt has been made to base an argument purely on the third article of faith, which was in fact rejected as a piece of rather sentimental existentialism.[5]

III

LAW AS AN EXPRESSION OF THE ORDINANCES OF CREATION

We may take as representations of this line of thought the two Lutherans, P. Althaus and W. Elert, as well as E. Brunner, a member of the Reformed Church. They, too, hold firmly to the belief that God's will, which is the ultimate standard for law, can only be known through revelation. But for these representatives of a natural theology this does not mean that God's will can only be known through holy scripture; for they hold that quite apart from the saving revelation of Jesus Christ, God has given an original testimony to himself in nature and history, a universal revelation from the beginning of all things. This "is not essentially bound up with faith . . . or with the bible story, but is natural, human and pre-Christian".[6] Brunner stresses the view that "the Christian idea of creation" compels us to recognize an element of revelation in the creative process; for what

[5] Cf. *Kirche und Recht.* A discussion on the Christian basis of law, initiated by the German Evangelical Church Assembly (Göttingen, 1950), p. 51.

[6] P. Althaus, *Die christliche Wahrheit I* (Gütersloh, 1947), p. 74.

kind of a creator would he be who did not stamp his creation with the impress of his spirit? [7] Man is aware of this natural revelation in his conscience and in his reflections upon his own existence. This view makes it possible for Brunner, in his book entitled *Righteousness* (1943), when dealing with the destruction of the Western conception of justice, to link up his thought with the traditions of the ancient world, and more particularly with Aristotle.

This approach makes it clear that law is based upon the order of existence expressed in creation. Brunner stresses the fact that God's will does not come to us in a sense of obligation that transcends existence, but in the very stuff of existence itself.[8] Although God is not the immanent world-logos, but the world lawgiver, the world's law is nevertheless a "manifestation of his creative will. . . . Behind the *suum cuique* stands the original divine order, which lays down what is proper for each person, the will of the creator, the order of creation".[9] For Althaus, law, together with marriage, nationality, the State and economics, belongs to the ordinances of creation, by which he understands "the indispensable conditions of the human life as lived on the plane of history", implanted in mankind by the creator through instinct and reason.[10]

Althaus sees these ordinances, in accordance with the Lutheran tradition of actualism, as historically variable entities, for "God's action does not establish one single abstract ordinance as such, but a number of concrete forms of ordinance; not a static and ready-made world, with natural, eternal and immutable forms of ordinances, but a dynamic world, pressing constantly forward to the creation of new forms". This statement is tinged with the same ambivalence that was already observable in Luther's idea of creation. On the one hand, he

[7] E. Brunner, *Die christliche Lehre von Gott* I (Zurich, 1946), p. 138.
[8] *Das Gebot und die Ordnungen* (Tübingen, 1933), pp. 109 and 192.
[9] *Gerechtigkeit*, 57. For Brunner, cf. I. H. Pohl, *Das Problem des Naturrechts bei Emil Brunner* (Zurich-Stuttgart, 1963) (Studien z. Dogmengesch. u. system. Theol. 17).
[10] *Theologie der Ordnungen*, [2]1935, pp. 9ff.

maintained that God's creation (*creare*) is an eternal activity, but at the same time the result of this activity (*creatum*).[11] Therefore, it is in keeping with Lutheran tradition for the idea of creation to be set out not in static and Platonic terms, as an eternal order of being, but as an historical and dynamic process.

This leads to a certain remoteness from the classical conception of natural law, as well as an approximation to the ordinances that are valid in the historical present. Here is where the weakness of this position starts, for at this point ideologizing and politicizing theory so easily creeps into the theological edifice. Althaus is thus well aware that these ordinances are necessarily shot through with sin, and that therefore "their particular historical form at any given moment must be critically examined to see whether they are in keeping with the divine intention behind the ordinances".[12] But he states most emphatically that "their meaning is not to be seen simply in the courting of the chaos which has arisen from human sin", and that they could therefore not simply be described as ordinances for preserving the *status quo,* or belonging to the Noachian dispensation. Hence marriage in Paul's view is not only a remedy for sin, but an original ordinance governing the relationship between the sexes, and the State is not only a *remedium peccati,* but an original ordinance designed to give men care and protection. Brunner lays stronger stress than Althaus on the normative significance of these ordinances. They are not simply orbits *within* which we have to act, but ordinances *according to* which we must shape our conduct, because in them men are confronted by God's will.[13] In the book entitled *Righteousness,* this normative function is even more strongly emphasised.

The other supporter of the Lutheran tradition, W. Elert, also speaks of natural ordinances (marriage, the family, the

[11] Cf. D. Löfgren, *Die Theologie der Schöpfung bei Luther* (Göttingen, 1960). Löfgren certainly tends to pass over the thoughts concerning creation in Luther because he also interprets God's actions *qua* redeemer and *qua* reconciler as different modes of his creative activity.

[12] *Ibid*, p. 29.

[13] *Das Gebet und die Ordnungen*, p. 275.

nation and the State) which "belong to the order of creation governed purely by natural law",[14] and form a permanent framework of existence in which God as "creator and ruler of the world . . . sets the life of mankind".[15] We are only concerned here with the creative and controlling actions of God the lawgiver. This level of existence, however, is not yet normative, for above it there is a second level of ordinances, a framework of obligation "which provides the material for showing the right and the wrong uses" of these natural ordinances. God's relation to them is that of a lawgiver, and this comparison leads Elert to elaborate the juridical analogy and go on to say that God's relationship to men is that of a judge who holds them accountable for their actions. Elert only allows the concept of natural law a limited importance; he compares it in particular with the decalogue, convicting man of his opposition to God (cf. Rom. 2).

The problem of ordinances has also been discussed in present-day Lutheran circles in terms of a different nomenclature, under the doctrine of the two kingdoms. In the kingdom of the world, God rules by force and by the sword, but in the kingdom of grace he rules by the Spirit and by his Word. It was precisely this doctrine that gave theologians a pretext for proclaiming the autonomy of the moral subject in the sphere of secular activities, and the independence of the rules that apply to it. That is why this teaching has come under particularly heavy criticism. In spite of the differences of detail to be found in their expositions—of which the two articles by Althaus and Heckel in the *Evang. Kirchenlexikon*[16] are an instructive example—there is a common recognition of one particular point—namely, that God is Lord of both kingdoms, and that only the form of

---

[14] *Das christliche Ethos* (Tübingen, 1949), p. 113.
[15] *Ibid.*, p. 82.
[16] In the article "Doctrine of the Two Kingdoms" by F. Althaus and J. Heckel (Göttingen, 1959), 1928-1936; cf. also J. van Laarhoven, "The Origin of Luther's Doctrine of the Two Kingdoms," in *Concilium* 17: Historical Investigations (Glen Rock, N.J.: Paulist Press, 1966), pp. 50-62.

his government is different in Church and State. Even if God's actions in the kingdom of the world are different in form from those in the kingdom of grace, this must not be allowed to lead to a double moral standard, for in both kingdoms all honor is due to God. It has indeed been put forward as a criticism of Luther that in his teaching he was at this point somewhat to blame,[17] for, like Calvin, he did not advise us sufficiently "how these two kingdoms form part of a whole".[18]

IV

THE BASIS OF LAW IN THE DOCTRINE OF GOD'S PRESERVATIVE ORDINANCES

The most difficult problem for the secular philosophy of law is the relationship between the timeless norm and the historical flux of legal conceptions. For the Evangelical basis of law, this connection is seen in the estrangement of historical man from the original ordinances through the agency of sin. This has had a disturbing effect both on the existence of man and on his capacity to recognize the disturbance; for if the reality of this estrangement is taken seriously, both the notion of an order of being that has remained intact and the notion of an intact reason by which it may be recognized necessarily collapse. And even "if we let the idea of such objective ordinances stand", our case is not much better, for they only become relevant for us men "if we recognize them and somehow behave toward them with understanding".[19]

The second variant of this theology of ordinances seeks to take these considerations into account. Its representatives are W. Künneth and H. Thielicke, to whom we might add the name of Father Gogarten, although he cannot be considered a typical

[17] E. Wolf, "Luthers Erbe?" in *Ev. Theol.* 6 (1946/47), pp. 82-114; printed in *Peregrinatio II* (Munich, 1965), pp. 58-81.
[18] K. Barth, *Rechtfertigung und Recht* (Zollikon-Zurich, ³1948), p. 4.
[19] H. H. Schrey, *Naturrecht und Gottesgerechtigkeit, Universitas* 5 (1950), p. 426.

representative of a theology of ordinance. In Künneth's view, the ordinances are not those originally established by the creator before the Fall, but his gracious ordinances for preservation, designed to save his creation from being left in the lurch, in spite of its estrangement from himself. These "ordinances of preservation" are the present form of God's creative activity in relation with a fallen world.[20] Even the administration of justice, fragmentary as it may be, is "a necessary service in support of God's preservative order".[21]

Thielicke's starting point is the view that sin brought about a total disruption of the whole cosmic order,[22] and this world is therefore to be regarded not "as supporting a divine order in harmony with the original creation, but as an aeon lying between the Fall and judgment". The State and the law are thus not a reflection of the creative order, but "structural forms of a fallen existence", and these primitive human ordinances therefore occupy a kind of twilight status, on the one hand thoroughly human, and on the other "a necessary orderly expression of the divine patience in maintaining and regulating a fallen world". Thus "the whole sphere of law, theologically speaking, expresses the way in which God comes to terms with a fallen humanity that is nevertheless in need of salvation because of the confusion created in this earth by reason of the Fall, in order that humanity shall not as it were bleed to death".[23] In a similar strain Gogarten can speak of "the State that takes its meaning and its reasoned basis from the protection of human existence in face of the power of evil that threatens it".[24]

D. Bonhoeffer lays particular emphasis upon the fact that these ordinances are not static—not ontological *ordines*—but arrangements or directions made by God, *ordinationes*. He would prefer the word *mandate* to that of ordinance. The bearer of a mandate acts as a representative who takes the place of

[20] *Politik zwischen Dämon und Gott* (Berlin, 1954), p. 139.
[21] *Ibid.*, p. 169.
[22] *Theologische Ethik,* I (Tübingen, 1951), pp. 698ff.
[23] *Ibid.*, III/3, p. 375.
[24] *Politische Ethik* (Jena, 1932), p. 213.

him by whom he is commissioned. If rightly understood, we could also make use of the concept of "ordinance", except that there is a danger of directing attention more to the existence of the order than to the God who alone gives it power and validity, legitimacy and authority. This can all too easily lead to giving divine sanction to all existing ordinances in general; from this it is but a short step to a romantic conservatism which has no connection at all with the four divine mandates.[25]

V

JUSTIFICATION AND JUSTICE—THE CHRISTOLOGICAL BASIS OF LAW

With Bonhoeffer we have in fact already made the transition to the next type of theological basis for law, for he finds the sole revelation of God's law in Jesus Christ and not in the powers of man's natural reason. This christological approach sees something wanting in the formal bases for law we have so far considered, because they are only concerned with the will of God as creator and sustainer, "whereas meanwhile God has done something new which overthrows all existing relationships—he has brought about the incarnation; but this is entirely ignored".[26] Yet, this line of thought is not concerned to sketch a "Christian law" that is only valid for Christians, for "law is in fact there for everyone, believers and unbelievers alike". However, it is intent upon showing that law belongs to a sphere in which Jesus Christ is king. This opens up an entirely different theological approach from that of the Lutheran "two-kingdom" doctrine, which proceeds from the difference between these two realms and traces back the norms of righteousness which are valid in this fallen world to the law of divine preservation, whereas Christ is Lord of the other and divine realm. Human

---

[25] *Ethik* (Munich, 1949), pp. 22ff. Bonhoeffer understands by the four divine mandates: law in the Church, marriage and the family, civilization, and secular authority.

[26] J. Ellul, *Die theologische Begründung des Rechtes* (Munich, 1949), p. 10.

and civic righteousness and righteousness in the sight of God are therefore two different kinds of righteousness, the one referring to the exterior, the other to the interior life of man.

At this point, Karl Barth, the chief proponent of the christological line of thought, asks whether this is a permissible distinction, and, in particular, whether it is to be taken as a hard and fast dividing line. "In what sense," he asks, "is it possible, permissible and even essential . . . to make a distinction, and yet to be obliged to speak in one and the same breath of 'divine and human righteousness'?" [27] Therefore, we are not concerned with an equation of the two kinds of righteousness; that would be the position taken up by the visionaries who already anticipate the coming kingdom of God and who seek to express the command to love one's neighbor in terms of law. But how does Barth view the connection? He does not see it in the form of two separate realms, but as two concentric circles with a common center in Jesus Christ, the Christian community being the inner circle and the community of citizens the outer one. But there exists both the possibility and the need for an affinity between them. "The righteousness of the State, as the Christian sees it, is constituted by its existence as a parable or form of correspondence or analogy with the kingdom of God believed in and proclaimed by the Church." [28] Because the community of citizens possesses this secret center, it does not have to fall back upon the "leaky cisterns" of natural law, but has a standard set by Jesus Christ. To be sure, the community of citizens does have to rely upon this questionable court of appeal constituted by natural law, or what they take to be and proclaim as such; yet, seen from the Christian point of view, this court of appeal can at most have the validity of a norm that is subordinate to an overriding norm, but can never itself have a normative force. This approach opens up very concrete norms of behavior. In particular, the community's inner order serves as model and

[27] K. Barth, *Rechtfertigung und Recht* (Zollikon-Zurich, ³1948), p. 3.
[28] *Christengemeinde und Burgergemeinde* (Stuttgart, 1946), p. 29 (Kirche für die Welt, 7).

example for the order of the world. Because Christ was concerned with men, the Christian community must also always
place the welfare of human beings in the forefront of its political
interests, rather than "causes" of any description,[29] even if these
causes should seek the welfare of the State, national honor or
cultural progress. The Christian community, as a witness for
righteousness—that is, for upholding and confirming the rights
of man in face of the attacks of sin and death—will "always
be found where the common order is based upon such a foundation that no one is excepted either from obedience to what is
recognized and received as law, or from the protection of this
law, and such that all political actions are in all circumstances
regulated by this law".

The French jurist, J. Ellul, after considering the various
covenants that God has made with mankind, comes to the conclusion that "the basis of law is to be found exclusively in Jesus
Christ".[30] Ellul conceives of law not in ontological categories,
but rather in terms of actualism and eschatology. God's will,
he maintains, is not an unbending principle from which a system
could be deduced. "It is always expressed in action and is in
strict correspondence with what the bible tells us about the
righteousness of God; it is only to be found in the act of judgment." [31] The full stature of this righteousness will only be seen
in the final judgment. These presuppositions lead Ellul to take
up a critical attitude to natural law, since "there is no law that
is inherent in the nature of man, for it is God alone who is the
source of right and law. This must therefore necessarily be
revealed, and not natural law".[32]

In the writings of the late J. Heckel we find an interesting
combination of the Lutheran teaching about the two kingdoms
and this christocratic basis of law. He starts from the idea of the
mystical body of Christ (*corpus Christi mysticum*), composed of

[29] *Ibid.*, p. 32.
[30] *Die theologische Begründung des Rechts* (Munich, 1948), p. 74
(Beiträge zur Evang. Theologie, 10).
[31] *Ibid.*, p. 34.
[32] *Ibid.*, p. 51.

both Church and State, over both of which Christ is Lord. The kingdom of this world stands in hostile opposition to this kingdom, for it is ruled by the devil. In this way Heckel combines the Augustinian dualism of the two mutually hostile kingdoms with the Lutheran conception of the two levels of rule and governance.[33]

VI

LAW AS RESTING UPON A SALVATION—HISTORICAL AND TRINITARIAN BASIS

The fourth approach to a theological basis for law, to which we now come, must be looked at as an attempt to overcome the one-sidedness of the views so far put forward. In 1949, an assembly of the German Evangelical Church was convened at Göttingen to discuss the Christian foundations of law.[34] It was joined in the following years by ecumenical conferences, which dealt with the same theme.[35] One was held at Treysa in 1950. The second thesis of the Göttingen findings contains the statement that "law as the basic constituent of human existence is rooted in the fact that God is the creator of man". But from the standpoint of salvation history this statement is seen both in connection with man's breach of law as regards God and his justification in Christ. The realm of *iustitia civilis*—that is, God's preservative ordinances—was regarded as the realm of God's "strange" work of justice, and it was not put on the same level

[33] Cf. J. Heckel, *Lex charitatis*. Eine juristische Untersuchung über das Recht in der Theologie M. Luthers (Munich, 1953) (Abhandlungen d. Bayer. Akademie d. Wiss., Phil.-hist. Kl. H. 36); also cf. a criticism of it by P. Althaus, "Luthers Lehre von den beiden Reichen im Feuer der Kritik," in *Luther-Jahrbuch* 24 (1957), pp. 40ff.

[34] The reviews, reports of proceedings and subjects dealt with in the Göttingen conference have been collected in a volume entitled *Kirche und Recht* (Göttingen, 1950).

[35] *Die Treysa-Konferenz 1950* über das Thema "Gerechtigkeit in biblischer Sicht", by the study section of the Church's Ecumenical Council (Geneva, 1950); cf. also H. H. Walz and H. H. Schrey, *Gerechtigkeit in biblischer Sicht* (Zürich-Frankfurt, 1955).

as God's "proper" work of "righteousness". In spite of this tendency to make the Lutheran distinction between the two realms,
there is then an emphatic statement that the law must not be
understood as a "principle" in isolation from the Gospel, for
this can be clearly seen to lead to modern totalitarian perver-
sions in secular society. The connection between the first and
second articles of belief, as well as the link with the process of
making actual laws, is provided by the fifth thesis which affirms
that the fact of man's creation and redemption is the source of
respect for human beings, which is a basic element in all proper
law and order.

At Treysa a similar line was adopted, and in particular the
noetic significance of the christology was brought out—that is,
its significance for discovering the true character of law. "All
our knowledge of the character, origins, validity and function
of human law springs from the belief in the Gospel of Jesus
Christ." Yet, even this statement does not lead on to the construction of a Christian law, but to an endeavor "to determine
the shape of human actions in the light of the lordship of Jesus
Christ, which is both to come and yet active even now in hidden
ways, and in the light of the final goal and end of time".[36]

To this series of attempts we should add the reflections on
the idea of the institution produced by the Commission on Marriage set up by the German Evangelical Church.[37] Here, too,
an attempt was made to produce a synthesis between historical
variability and ontological continuity by defining the institution
as "a juridical expression of typical forms of relationship, which
can indeed be largely embodied in forms, but are initially 'given'
and basically beyond human control".

We have now come to the end of this attempt to depict the
most important approaches to a new theological basis for law
among Evangelical Christians. In spite of the differences in detail, a common direction is nevertheless observable. There is a

[36] Wolf, "Zum protestantischen Rechtsdenken," in *Perigrinatio II* (Munich, 1965), p. 206.
[37] Collected in *Recht und Institution* (Witten, 1956); cf. also R. P.
Calliess, *Eigentum als Institution* (Munich, 1962).

common endeavor to rescue the fundamental question of law
from the old and sterile alternatives of natural law or positivism
and "to make a bold attempt to break through to new ground
beyond natural law and positivism, where the tensions between
them, if not removed, might at any rate be lessened".[38] This
attempt is ecumenically important because it comes from the
heart of biblical faith and leads toward the solution not only of
a traditional problem, but also of a question that is a burning
issue for the present time.

[38] Quoted from E. Wolf, "Rechtfertigung und Recht," in *Kirche und
Recht,* 23; cf. also K. Ritter, *Zwischen Naturrecht und Rechtspositivismus*
(Witten, 1956) (= Glaube und Forschung, 10); H. H. Schrey, "Recht,
christl. Begründung," in *Evang. Soziallexikon* (Stuttgart, ⁴1965), 1005-
1009.

Stanley Kutz, C.S.B./*Toronto, Canada*

Reflections on the
Virtue of Truthfulness

W hat one may say about the virtue of truthfulness in any given age or culture will depend very greatly upon the nature of the epistemological principles and presuppositions that underlie the conscious attempts at communication in that era or culture. This fact makes it very difficult to reflect on the virtue of truthfulness at the present moment, for it is precisely an epistemological revolution which is at the heart of the current renewal of Catholic life and theology.[1] The following attempts at such reflection will make very little sense to anyone whose sensitivity is not awakened to the central importance of the epistemological question in the search for an adequate conceptualization of the "new life" which the Catholic community is undoubtedly experiencing.

It seems to me that the traditional manner of conceptualizing the process whereby truth is perceived and communicated is somewhat as follows (allowance being made for oversimplification): Truth is perceived when the mind of the "subject" receives a faithful impression or representation of an "object" which exists outside the mind. Truthfulness consists in the accurate

---

[1] This fact has been brilliantly demonstrated in the recently published study of my colleague, Professor L. Dewart, entitled *The Future of Belief* (Herder & Herder: New York, 1966). Unfortunately, this book came into my hands only after the present essay was completed, and I was unable to incorporate Dewart's insights to the degree I would have wished.

expression of the received representation, by word or gesture, in such a manner that it can be received intact by the eyes, ears and mind of other persons. Briefly, the process of perceiving and communicating truth was understood on the analogy of the sending-receiving process which takes place in the transmission of sound waves via radio.[2]

Implicit in this view is an epistemology which takes our knowledge of *things,* of physical realities, as the model of all knowledge, including even our knowledge of persons and of personal qualities and dispositions.[3] A consequence of this view is that truth comes to be thought of in terms of an *objectified possession,* and the norms governing the retention and transmission of this "possession" have tended to become assimilated to the laws governing the possession and exchange of property.

This way of regarding truth and the virtue of truthfulness was useful enough in an era which concurred in accepting the objectified world-view which was implied in it. But it becomes increasingly less useful as human consciousness rises to that level where consciousness itself (subjectivity and intersubjectivity) becomes the "eye" through which the world is contemplated. Contemporary man is less inclined to look upon his knowledge as an accumulation of facts or truths which he may give or sell to others at his own discretion, or in accordance with claims which they may make upon him; he is more inclined to look upon his knowledge as being of a piece with his very consciousness, his self, his personhood, and to regard the process of sharing it with others as involving a personal relationship,

[2] The inadequacy of the transmitter-receiver analogy for the conceptualization of our perception of truth is best demonstrated by G. Marcel in *The Mystery of Being,* I (Reflection and Mystery: Gateway Edition, 1960, pp. 127-133. Originally published by The Harvill Press, Great Britain, 1950. English translation by G. S. Fraser (= Le Mystère de l'Etre: Paris, Aubier, 1961).

[3] See E. Schillebeeckx, *Christ, the Sacrament of the Encounter with God* (Sheed & Ward: London, 1963), p. 3. See also Cornelius Ernst's Foreword to the same volume, p. xv. Originally published as *Christus, sacrament van de Godsontmoeting,* [8]1965. Translated into English by Paul Barrett *et al.*

a revealing and a giving of himself to another, rather than as a sort of commercial transaction which never gets beyond an exchange of things or commodities.

In some areas of our lives, this change in viewpoint with respect to the nature of truth is not likely to entail any significant change in our practical expression of the virtue of truthfulness. As social beings, we recognize that a peaceful and creative living-together requires that our social intercourse be governed by a high degree of truthfulness and reliability in our day-to-day communication with each other. Even in this area, of course, it will make for greater personal maturity and social harmony if the virtue of truthfulness is regarded as a personal service which we wish to offer our fellowman for the enrichment of our life in common, rather than as a "right" that society (which tends to be conceived impersonally) can demand of us (on the analogy of the right of eminent domain).

Actually, in this area of the relationship of the individual to society, one wonders if there is not more need, in the age of computers, lie detectors and electronic "snoopers", for an insistence on the rights of privacy than on the obligation of truthfulness. It is quite possible that the degree of truthfulness which is essential for the smooth functioning of public life will one day be assured by technology and removed from the area of free choice. In fact, this development is already well underway. It becomes less and less possible for the citizen to be anything but "truthful" with the tax-collector, the judge and a host of other agents of the society in which he lives.

Whether one welcomes these developments or views them with alarm, it seems clear that they will have the effect of providing us with a different focus for our reflections on the virtue of truthfulness. Instead of being principally concerned with veracity in the reporting of facts, we shall have to become more concerned with fidelity to self in self-expression and self-revelation.

This development, I believe, will demand of us a real deepening of our understanding of the virtue of truthfulness. It will force us to become more nuanced and critical in our reflection upon the quality and variety of our personal relationships, and the degree of self-revelation that is appropriate to them. Conversely, it will allow us, perhaps, to be more direct and frank in our expression of the rights of privacy which are appropriate to our condition as persons.

With respect to this last point, we might reflect for a moment on the so-called "mental reservation". The very existence of such a category in our moral thinking and the fact that we have developed a fairly sophisticated casuistry around it are evidence of our instinctive awareness of a natural right to a certain degree of personal privacy. It is clear that not everyone has a right to know "whether I am at home" or "whether I am busy" or "what I am doing next week" at any moment that he may choose to call on me.

But most of us feel somewhat ill at ease with the dissimulations which our handbooks of moral theology recommend in these situations.[4] This, I believe, is because we tend to view truth as a commodity which we have somehow placed on the public market by the very fact that we are members of a society. Hence we feel that anyone who offers the right price (by asking a question) is entitled to a portion of our commodity. Even when we are convinced that it was tactless of him to ask the question, we still feel uncomfortable if we give a dissimulating answer (= a fraudulent product).

Now if we come to regard truthfulness more in terms of a mode of personal self-expression, I believe we shall be able to protect our privacy in such situations more effectively and with a better conscience. We shall realize that the mere asking of a question does not entitle the questioner to a direct answer, on a *quid pro quo* basis. We shall recognize as well that the *expressed* question does not always convey the *real* question or

---

[4] The handbooks, in their examples, often interpose a third party (secretary or maid) between the questioner and the victim. This has the effect of reducing the moral discomfort of all three parties. Unfortunately, most people cannot count on the services of a secretary or maid in these situations.

the real intent of the questioner. By becoming more sensitive to the real needs of the questioner and the quality of his relationship to us, we will be enabled to be more imaginative and creative in our mode of response, and we may find more options available to us than a direct answer on the one hand, or a dissimulating "mental reservation" on the other.

It seems to me that this is the manner in which Jesus ordinarily expressed himself and communicated with people. He did not feel constrained to answer questions directly, least of all when they were unjustified or implied unreasonable or unhealthy requests. Sometimes he responded with a question of his own (as when the mother of James and John requested special privileges for her sons in the kingdom, and Jesus replied with a question which revealed the true nature of the kingdom and the inappropriateness of the request). Often he responded with a parable which, while avoiding or postponing a direct answer to the question asked, was nevertheless a more appropriate response to the person asking. And on one occasion he seems to have spoken a deliberate "untruth". His brethren asked him if he were going up to a festival in Jerusalem (to display his miracles). He replied: "I do not go up to this festival." Later, in fact, he did go. It seems to me much simpler and more accurate to understand Jesus' answer in this instance as the appropriate personal response to the unenlightened expectations of his brethren than to attempt to rationalize it in terms of a mental reservation.

Seen in this light, it becomes clear that the most *truthful* answer to a question (that is, the one which is the best response to the *person* of the questioner) will not in every case be the most *factual* answer. Indeed, the merely factual answer can often be a way of keeping the questioner at a distance, or leaving him in his ignorance, instead of becoming a means of true communication and communion with him. But it is difficult for us to be sensitive to this nuanced understanding of truthfulness so long as we adhere to an "objectified" epistemology and theory of communication. The parables of Jesus are a source of confusion and even a scandal to the person who expects truth to be expressed only in clearly defined concepts and judgments, and whose model of human communication is drawn from the court-room or the marketplace.

What becomes apparent from the mode of communication employed by Jesus is that truth and the obligation of truthful-ness are incumbent not only on the speaker but on the hearer as well. Truth can only "happen" where there is an openness to communication on the part of at least two persons. It would be literally (if only partially) true to say that "truth is in the ear of the hearer"—or as Jesus put it: "He who has ears to hear, let him hear." The reason there is so little truth in our life and our world is not so much that the truth does not get spoken, but that it does not get *heard*. The number of people who make a policy of conscious and deliberate prevarication has probably never been very great in the history of civilization, but there seem to be a great many people who have a "hearing" problem—the uncircumcised of heart and ear, in the biblical phrase. Per-haps as we come to understand that the moral virtue of truth-fulness must first of all be cultivated by virtuous listening, we shall also begin to make more progress in speaking the truth and doing the truth.

We ought not to imagine that what has just been said about hearing the truth applies only to profound religious or "spiritual" truth, or to intimate I-Thou relationships. Psychological studies have amply demonstrated the fact that the accuracy with which people perceive even the simplest factual truths can be greatly diminished by their momentary emotional state or by their more permanent psychic predispositions. This impaired "hearing" will lead, naturally, to an impaired "speaking" of the truth. No doubt many instances of "untruthfulness" ought to be understood not in terms of a culpable moral lapse on the part of the speaker, but rather as an inevitable consequence of his stunted or dis-torted ability to hear and to perceive the truth.

The fact that we can ascribe some (or much) of the untruth in the world to the influence of unculpable psychic predispositions or distortions which diminish the ability to hear the truth does not permit the moral theologian or the pastor to absolve himself of concern for these phenomena. Untruth is still an evil, whether it is culpable or not. Whether it proceeds from conscious motives or from unconscious dispositions, it will still bring frustration and unhappiness to the person afflicted with it and to all those in contact with him. Indeed, the untruth which proceeds from psychopathological influences is likely to have far more destructive effects than conscious and culpable deception. For the latter can be unmasked and coped with by the ordinary man, whereas the former can usually be identified and treated only by a professional psychotherapist. If our moral theology and our pastoral practice are concerned with the real healing (*salus*) of man, and not merely with judging his conscious delinquencies, they will have to concern themselves more and more with problems of this sort, and will have to ally themselves more closely with those healing arts which deal directly with the unconscious and the emotions. This, of course, is necessary for a deeper understanding and a more effective pedagogy not only of the virtue of truthfulness, but of every other virtue as well.

Léonce Hamelin, O.F.M. / *Montreal, Canada*

Communications Media at the Service of "Good Morals"

The media of social communication constitute a thorny problem provoking endless study and debate. They continually propagate values and ideologies, and create desires demanding a choice. This choice is rendered all the more difficult to the extent that the moral sense of the people has been deadened. Only yesterday, men in general were obedient to tradition. Each society possessed a vision of the world that was handed on from generation to generation; each people had its culture which provided for the conduct of the individual in every circumstance of life. Such a synthesis is nowadays impossible. Men are now seeking intuitive values which they do not succeed in defining.

The communications media have come in for a good deal of praise. As resources stemming from the goodness of the creator, they present the world with an unparalleled opportunity for disseminating information and culture, reaching all men, even in the most remote regions. Yet experience demonstrates the dangers posed by these same instruments.

Hence, the Church, as the continuer of Christ's mission to proclaim the message of salvation, has for a long time insisted that the moral order must always be respected: "Public authority, which legitimately concerns itself with the health of the citizenry, is obliged, through the promulgation and careful enforcement of

83

laws, to exercise a fitting and careful watch lest grave damage befall *public morals* [or *good morals*] and the welfare of society through the base use of these media." [1]

"Good morals" represents a term that has been abused for some time and repeated indefinitely without very much consideration given to the meaning it might shelter. In no case can we discover an official meaning for it. Obviously borrowed from juridic language, the expression is not further defined by jurists. [2] In the extensive literature on the media of communication, especially the cinema, we find nothing in the way of a better definition. And during this time the contemporary world inclines more and more to easy pleasure. Everything that would seem to restrain freedom has been swept away in order to remain on the level of a social morality. This does not simplify the problem.

What then are "good morals"? We believe the meaning of the expression is in the process of a complete evolution which we will analyze on the level of three different interpretations.

I

TRADITIONAL PHILOSOPHICAL INTERPRETATION

Pontifical documents prior to the *Pastoral Constitution on the Church in the Modern World* (*Gaudium et spes*) leave no possible doubt concerning the identification of "good morals" with natural morality. *Vigilanti cura, Miranda prorsus,* and the conciliar *Decree on the Media of Social Communication* (*Inter mirifica*)—to cite only the most important—suffice to demonstrate this point. For example, this last document makes indifferent use of "moral law" (n. 6), "norms of morality" (n. 5), "faith or good morals" (n. 10), and "public morals" (n. 12). The Italian bishops, in their collective letter on the morality of the cinematographic form, neglect the term and employ a more

---

[1] *Decree on the Media of Social Communication,* n. 12.
[2] Cf. A. Bride, "Bonnes moeurs," in *Catholicisme* II, pp. 150-1.

comprehensive expression: the cinema must "submit itself to an objective moral law inspired by the very nature of man".[3]

The commentators—at least those familiar to us—do not furnish a definition of terms; they adduce a description which also identifies this term with natural morality. Thus Ludmann, speaking of "good morals", enumerates the virtues of order, loyalty, goodness and justice,[4] somewhat as Le Senne had spoken of nobility, fidelity, purity, plenitude and strength of soul as radiations of moral value.[5] Both civil and canon law also limit the extension of the term to the imperatives of the natural law concerning honesty, justice and equity.[6]

The point of departure for such an identification is found at least partly in the natural manner of acting on the part of peoples. For every society manifests a corpus of unsystematized rules which in a popular way determine how to behave in the different circumstances of life. In this way, "good morals" becomes an empirical notion which describes the attitude of an honorable man. Thus, the morality of an honorable man—we should say "simple morality"—corresponds to a manner of acting inspired by common opinion prior to any philosophical considerations.

Nevertheless, in asking us to respect "good morals", the Church surely does not have in mind these popular sociological patterns of behavior. This would be tantamount to canonizing mores which from the viewpoint of morality often need reforming. First, such patterns of behavior are not the same everywhere; secondly, the sensitivity of peoples varies tolerably with the ages.[7]

For its part, philosophical thought is seeking a concept of nature in order eventually to formulate a definite rule of conduct

---

[3] Published at Rome on March 20, 1961.

[4] R. Ludmann, *Cinéma, foi et morale* (Coll. Recontres, 46) (Paris, 1956), p. 21.

[5] R. Le Senne, *Traité de Morale générale* (Paris, 1949), pp. 710-1.

[6] Cf. A. Bride, *op. cit.*

[7] Cf. J. Leclercq, *Saisir la vie à pleines mains*. Un traité de morale (Paris, 1961), p. 170.

in conformity to it. But what is man? In order to answer this question we must at all costs consider him within the totality of his reality and take into account his experience of a certain order of values. Utilizing concrete data, the philosophical considerations terminate in an ensemble of moral dispositions and superior values which lay the foundation for the establishment of the concept of nature. The "good morals" thus become the expression of nature in common attitudes defining natural morality.[8]

Traditional among philosophers,[9] this notion has served theologians as an approach to the formulation of their morals. "It is appropriate," Monsignor Delhaye will declare, "for Christians not to look askance at this morality; it enables them to conduct a dialogue with non-Christians and establish a rather complete familial, social and political morality common to all."[10] The presence of natural morality is also emphasized in biblical morality, which confirms the assertion of theologians.[11]

It was therefore entirely normal for pontifical documents to identify "good morals" with this natural morality formulated by philosophers and ratified by theologians.

II

CONTEMPORARY PHENOMENOLOGICAL INTERPRETATION

The preceding notion encounters difficulty in finding acceptance nowadays, at least in the static sense so long accorded

[8] Cf. O. Lottin, *Morale fondamentale* (Coll. Bibliothèque de Theol., 1) (Tournai, 1954), pp. 110-1; B. Häring, *La loi du Christ* I (Tournai, 1957), pp. 359-60.
[9] Cf. Ph. Delhaye, *Permanence du droit naturel* (Coll. Analecta Medaevalia Namurcensia, 10) (Louvain/Lille/Montreal, 1962).
[10] *Ibid.*, p. 127.
[11] See, among others, C. Spicq, *Théologie morale du N.T.* (Coll. Etudes Bibl., I) (Paris, 1965), pp. 394ff.; I. Husik, "The Law of Nature, Hugo Grotius, and the Bible," in *Hebrew Union College Annual* 2 (1925), pp. 394-417; A. N. Wilder, "Equivalents of Natural Law in the Teaching of Jesus," in *The Journal of Religion* 15 (1945), pp. 125-35; E. Hamel, "Loi naturelle et loi du Christ," in *Sc. Eccl.* 10 (1958), pp. 49-76; Ph. Delhaye, *op. cit.*, pp. 31ff., 115ff.; P. Grelot, *Sens chrétien de l'A.T.* (Paris, 1962), pp. 175ff.

it. Until the end of the 19th century, civilization had been built up on a notion of nature sufficiently solid to establish a kind of stable fortification around each generation. But from about 1880 onward, science, technology and philosophy have gradually whittled away this reassuring image. The Bergsonian dynamism first contests the rights of the intelligence and reason; then the existential phenomenologies succeed in dismantling the structures of rational knowledge. The ancient universality of human nature, envisaged in the abstract, gives way to the study of particular contingent situations which condition our behavior.

Sensitive to these considerations, theologians have agreed to revise their position—at first with some hesitation[12] and later with progressively more reassurance.[13] The Church now upholds these new views. Theology—like philosophy—had been ever searching for a universal man; we are obliged to affirm today that such an abstract being is never encountered.

Today it is more difficult to form a synthesis of the various disciplines of knowledge and the arts than it was formerly. For while the mass and the diversity of cultural factors are increasing, there is a decrease in each man's faculty of perceiving and unifying these things, so that the image of "universal man" is being lost sight of more and more. Nevertheless it remains each man's duty to preserve an un-

[12] Cf. Ph. Delhaye, op. cit., p. 18: "Existentialists are not absolutely wrong when they protest against a certain conception of human nature which makes an a priori idea insensitive to the evolution of history. Such a nature certainly exists as a common basis among men, but on this basis there are a thousand individual variations that must be taken into consideration even in morality."

[13] Cf. M. Oraison, Pour une morale de notre temps (Paris, 1964), pp. 37ff.; I. Lepp, La morale nouvelle (Paris, 1963), pp. 80-100; K. Rahner, Ecrits théologiques III (Tournai/Paris, 1963), pp. 15-6: "We always think of the abstract nature of man inevitably with regard to the model man offered to us by experience. But until the end of his history man will never completely know what is his nature and what is its model in simple fact. Every history of the mind of man bears witness to this. For he is continually learning new modes of realization of his unique being which he could never have deduced a priori from his essence. And by means of these new modes he experiences the difference between essence and concrete historical realization which formerly he had regarded as one more or less indissoluble synthesis."

derstanding of the whole human person in which the values of intellect, will, conscience and fraternity are preeminent. These values are all rooted in God the creator and have been wonderfully restored and elevated in Christ.[14]

We are continually confronted with two realities in this task of reflection, and we must respect their laws. On the one hand, in the Pauline view, every man—no matter in how confused a manner—knows his moral duty and tends toward its fulfillment; this is what makes him a responsible being. On the other hand, although this moral vision is absolute and universal, it is formulated historically in a contingent and provisional way.

The differences in morals, which are at times quite considerable, are thus explained by man's freedom regarding the manner of making his natural moral vision conform to his rule of behavior; a morality with the compelling force of an instinct would no longer be a "morality", in the sense that it would no longer rest on man's freedom. The mode of perceiving what constitutes the good in concrete circumstances varies among men and depends a good deal on the situation and the socio-cultural milieu.

It is by means of all these factors that we must—with difficulty—discover constant values. This is only right, for the absence of evident determination in human beings about what constitutes the good in concrete situations causes moral values to be the object of a continual adjustment. Hence, there is need for a real dialogue with all men of goodwill, evolving to the rhythm of a world in transformation. These considerations lead to the formulation of a new morality with the principal characteristics of independence from all determinism and a pronounced tendency toward freedom. The difficulties of forming minds in such a morality are already foreshadowed.[15]

[14] *Pastoral Constitution on the Church in the Modern World*, n. 61.
[15] The anxiety raised by this problem of school-formation is reencountered in several contemporary documents. They do not regulate the problem, but they can at last shed light on it. Cf. *Half Our Future*. A Report of the Central Advisory Council for Education (England), Her Majesty's Stationery Officer, 1963; *General Education in a Free Society*. Report of the Harvard Committee (Harvard University Press, 1962);

It is to this effort that the Church is presently applying herself. In our day, the theologian must be "evolutionary",[16] that is to say, capable of an authentic fidelity at one and the same time to the message of God, the dignity of the human person and the values discovered by our age. Even non-Christians participate more or less profoundly in revelation. This accounts for the fact that formulations are always subject to revision in a common effort at continued refinement.

To ask the communications media to be the guarantors of "good morals" is to require that they be "instruments at the service of a truly universal examination of conscience".[17] What can be said of this? In the most immediate sense, to reimpart to the pontifical texts a touch of modernity one would have to say that "good morals" are to be identified with this new natural morality which is in process of discovery. This still leaves the problem of its imprecisions. Hence, to be better understood, theologians continue to emphasize their refusal to identify *morality* and *science of mores*.[18] They thus retain for the term "good

General Education in School and College. A Committee Report by the Members of the Faculties of Andover, Lawrenceville, Harvard, Princeton and Yale (Harvard University Press, 1964); *Development of Moral and Spiritual Values through the Curriculum of California High Schools* (California State Department of Education, 1952); *Moral and Spiritual Values in Education* (Los Angeles City School Publication, n. 580: Revised edition, 1954); *Programmes et instruction commentées* (Enseignement élémentaire, par MM. Lebattre et Verney) (Paris: Editions Bourrelier, 1962); *Rapport de la Commission Royale d'enquête sur l'enseinement dans la Province de Québec,* t. III (Deuxième partie du rapport) (Quebec, 1965), pp. 205-33.

[16] I. Lepp (*op. cit.,* p. 89) writes "revolutionary", but he explains the sense of his term: "In this sense all authentic morality is necessarily *revolutionary,* evidently on condition that the word revolution be understood dialectically, the accent being placed not on the overthrow and destruction of what is but on the creation of what should be."

[17] *Ibid.,* p. 98.

[18] *Ibid.,* pp. 92-3: "In refusing the notion of a static and immutable human nature . . . we are not in any way tempted by the theories of the sociological school, identifying morality with the science of mores. The science of mores merely takes inventory of the given state of mores in a given society, at any given time." For his part, J. Leclercq refuses to confuse morality and moral (*op. cit.,* pp. 170-2), but according to him *science of mores* and *moral science* are two expressions referring to the

morals" the sense of simple morality which we have defined above.

However, the difficulties raised by such a position can easily be foreseen. For the man in the street, the expression no longer practically signifies anything. The values which concretely guarantee the dignity of the human person are not sufficiently designated therein. Better defined data are needed.

III

PROPOSED PASTORAL INTERPRETATION

What meaning, then, must be given to "good morals" so that the term can still speak to our contemporaries? It would be illusory to think that the moral authority enjoyed by the Church continues to have enough power to direct the communications media toward good, and even more illusory to believe that condemnation suffices to cause everyone to submit docilely. In order to exert any influence, it is necessary to know how to carry on a dialogue with those in charge of these same media.

Various observations can enable us to identify the qualities which should mark this dialogue and assure "good morals". We are not seeking herein a definition, but rather a valid prudential attribute for the producer who completes his work as well as for the consumer who must make a judgment concerning it. Amédée Ayfre leads us along this path. His analysis concerns art, and, in a

---

same thing: "This new art of living is called *science of mores* or *moral science,* but the newness of the words and methods should not deceive us about the novelty of the thought. It is simply a case of the age-old morality of an honorable man presented with a scientific apparatus of observation which the ancients never thought of" (p. 158). He then goes on to identify this science of mores with natural morality (p. 159). In order to clear up the problem, we must make note of the fact that the moral question is situated on four levels: *morality:* simple popular morality (what is done); the *science of mores:* sociological morality (systematization of popular morality); *natural morality:* philosophical morality (universal morality in the process of evolution); *supernatural morality:* theological morality (the law of Christ). The term "good morals" can refer to the first three realities.

particular sense, the cinematographic art, but it can be applied with the necessary adjustments to the modern means of communication.[19]

The first observation calls our attention to the cultural value of the media of social communication. These exercise a profound influence on social mores, and this influence has often been analyzed.[20] But it is equally true to say that they are especially and primarily witnesses of the moral level of peoples.[21] Consequently, truth requires authenticity of the facts they report.

The second observation flows from the first. If, in order to be faithful to truth, those who use these media must appeal to descriptions which seem to attack "good morals", honesty recommends that they do so with a serious concern for the respect due the human person.[22] For we are all aware of the ambivalent use

[19] A. Ayfre, *Conversion aux images?* (Coll. 7e art. 39) (Paris, 1964). In the extensive literature dealing with the cinema, most of the authors unfortunately do little more than develop the subject. Among the better known works are C. Ford, *Le cinéma au service de la foi* (Coll. Présences) (Paris, 1953); R. Ludmann, *Cinéma, foi et morale* (Coll. Recontres, 46) (Paris, 1956); *Cinéma, Télévision et Pastorale* (Coll. Recherches pastorales, 7) (Paris, 1964); B. Häring, "Les techniques de diffusion et la communion des personnes dans la vérité et la beauté," in *op. cit.*, III, pp. 277-313; A. Fournel, "Le jugement moral et le cinéma," in *Lumière et Vie* 10 (1961), pp. 69-84.

[20] The influence exercised by the communications media has elicited a good deal of comment. For example, emphasis has been given to the reasons of a physical and psychological order that might explain the great attraction of the cinema, but the spheres of such influence have possibly not yet succeeded in being determined. Cf. A. Gemelli, "Cinéma et psychologie," in *Rev. Intern du Cinéma* 2 (1950), pp. 32ff.; *Cinéma, Télévision et Pastorale*, pp. 73-5.

[21] Cf. *Cinéma, Télévision et Pastorale*, pp. 27-8; R. Ludmann, *op. cit.*, pp. 17-8; *Pastoral Constitution on the Church in the Modern World*, nn. 61-62: "Literature and the arts are also, in their own way, of great importance to the life of the Church. They strive to make known the proper nature of man, his problems and his experiences in trying to know and perfect both himself and the world" (n. 62).

[22] This theme has often been brought up. The *Decree on the Media of Social Communication* summarizes the state of the problem: "Finally, the narration, description or portrayal of moral evil, even through the media of social communication, can indeed serve to bring about a deeper knowledge and study of humanity and, with the aid of appropriately heightened dramatic effects, can reveal and glorify the grand dimensions of truth and goodness. Nevertheless, such presentations ought always to be subject to

that can be made of the media of social communication. In the eyes of some they constitute a commercial product wherein all that matters is the product-consumer relationship, based on the law of supply and demand. Rare are those who regard these media as the means of expression of the human person with all the respect and exigencies this implies. The class of the elite is habitually suffering drastic reduction.

Finally, we should add—as our third observation—the point that a work always mirrors its author to some degree or other. Absolute objectivity does not exist; behind the word, image or sound, we can invariably perceive the person who produced it. Every expression—no matter what it might be—suggests something: "Even live programs, or the photos of *Paris-Match,* already orient the mind toward a certain idea of the event." [23] The concern of the creator must thus aim to go beyond the material reality and give it a meaning.

With the above observations as a basis, three qualities appear necessary for a work to be morally valid: sincerity, honesty and authenticity. First, *sincerity:* "A work is truly moral in its constitution only if it sincerely reflects the personality of the one or more authors responsible." Next, *honesty:* "Here it is a question of respecting what is spoken about, as well as those to whom one speaks." Finally, *authenticity:* "The film [the completed work] is authentic which succeeds, by the extreme coherence of signs and meaning, in revealing ideas whose truth imposes itself with evidence. On the contrary, the work is not authentic which, for lack of internal unity of meaning and form, purpose and method, seeks to appear more than it is or appears in slight or poor manner what it wishes to be." [24]

---

moral restraint lest they work to the harm rather than the benefit of souls, particularly when there is a question of treating matters which deserve reverent handling or which, given the baneful effect of original sin in men, could quite readily arouse base desires in them" (n. 7).

[23] A. Ayfre, *op. cit.,* p. 12.

[24] *Ibid.,* pp. 192-3. This should not be construed as a condemnation of the work of the Office Catholique du Cinéma. It has a role to play—informing consciences. But its action will be efficacious only insofar as it is inspired by the prudential attitude we have tried to define.

Doubtless, it is possible to reach a restrained agreement on the various values capable of defining "good morals"; however, one fact remains certain: respect for the elements that we have just enumerated assures at the same time respect for "good morals". "If the morality of art as art can constitute only one chapter of an integral human morality, it does not consist solely in the application of a few general principles to a particular case, but rather in the formulation—in the twofold light of values and facts—of a practice which really affects the very structures of this universe apart. . . . The moral significance of a work must first be drawn out for itself in reference to these few values which we have recognized as essential: sincerity, honesty and authenticity." [25]

On a good many points that raise difficulties, the Church has modified her attitude since Vatican Council II: nowadays, instead of condemning or proscribing, she proposes.[26] Why cannot moralists do as much? Instead of defining "good morals" and condemning those who do not correspond to their definitions, why do they not propose a prudential attitude?

Nevertheless, we should have no illusions! The transformation of the communications media will not occur tomorrow. For a long time to come we will still have among us journalists seeking popularity, television writers in search of a "rating" and screen writers in pursuit of the dollar—all at the expense of the true, the beautiful and the good. In spite of deceptive appearances, let us preserve the Church's firm hope, in the knowledge that perseverance in effort does not necessarily require constant success.

[25] *Ibid.*, pp. 198-9.
[26] Cf. *Pastoral Constitution on the Church in the Modern World*, n. 47.

PART II
BIBLIOGRAPHICAL
SURVEY

Coenraad van Ouwerkerk, C.SS.R./*Wittem, Netherlands*

Secularism and Christian Ethics: Some Types and Symptoms

At the present time there exist certain trends which, centered about the catchword "secularism", are having either direct or indirect repercussions upon Christian ethics. It is these trends I shall discuss here. "Secularism" is a vogue word and, in common with all such phenomena, unmistakably conveys a particular attitude to life. It is, on the other hand, so vague, and capable of so many interpretations, as to render a clear definition impossible.[1] Secularism and secularization refer to the process and task of estimating the true value of man and world within the framework of faith. However, they may also indicate the denial of any transcendence to God and consequently deny the presence of God in human existence and the possibility of a direct relationship with him.

Between these two extremes the field of theology embraces various so-called secular concepts and trends that have one common characteristic: the desire to come to grips with the situation of the Christian in the present-day world.

In view of the many interpretations attributed to the word

---

[1] Besides the definition of secularization in various dictionaries, cf. F. Gogarten, *Verhagnis und Hoffnung der Neuzeit*. Die Säkulariserung als theologisches Problem (Stuttgart, 1953). For Dutch readers, cf. C. van Peursen, "Functioneel Denken en geloof," in *Gemeente onderweg* (Lochem); M. Krinkels, "Sekularisering. Een poging tot begripsverheldering," in *Theologie en zielzorg* 62 (1966), pp. 265-74.

"secularism" and the multiplicity of trends bearing this name, it might be well to clarify the position by giving a concrete description of the various movements within modern secular theology and ethics.

We shall not attempt a chronological description of the various stages of secularism within Christian ethics. Their origin is often obscure and the various phases frequently overlap. Nor is it our intention to deal in this article with all the publications on this subject. The literature is only accessible to a limited degree, and the problems connected with secularism are legion. We have thus confined ourselves to certain types and symptoms, hoping nonetheless to obtain some picture of what is happening in this field in Christian ethics. The voices of the Reformed Churches will be heard most frequently, since the phenomenon of secularism within Christian ethics has been more often and more openly discussed by writers from these Churches. A certain secular mentality is undoubtedly present in Catholic thought, but it is not so clearly evidenced in writing; it emerges more in conversation and in oral discussion.

I

CATHOLIC MORAL THEOLOGY
CONFRONTED WITH THE PHENOMENON OF SECULARISM

It was not so long ago that Catholic moral theologians reacted against the excessively philosophical and profane tone of moral theology and opted for a specifically theological and, above all, christological ethic.[2] This christological reorientation forms only one aspect and one phase of the entire post-war renewal of moral theology,[3] but it is certainly the most striking and the most far-reaching. We see the development of a first, deliberate confronta-

[2] Still a classic in this respect is Fr. Tillmann's *Die Idee der Nachfolge Christi* (Handbuch der Katholischen Sittenhehre, III) (Dusseldorf, 1934).
[3] To name only a few descriptions of the trends in moral theology: G. Thils, *Tendences actuelles en théologie morale* (Gembloux, 1940); F. Böckle, "Bestrebrungen in der Moraltheologie," in *Fragen der Theologie heute* (Einsiedeln, 1957), pp. 425-66; J. Ford and G. Kelly, *Contemporary*

tion with the natural sciences, and an open-minded approach to the *realités terrestres*. At the same time, however, and, it seems to me, with no suggestion of contradiction or inconsistency, an un-ambiguous stand is taken on the theological norms and the essentially Christian content of moral theology. For these authors the Christian character of the ethical life can clearly be defined intrinsically, and may be taken as the obvious criterion in es-tablishing any norm. The Christian code is self-evident: it is that of the world which gives rise to problems. A system of ethics founded on grace is contrasted with one based on the natural law, and that sometimes with such partiality and a tendency toward supranaturalism that L. Buys in the 1940's felt obliged to sound a warning against "evangelical puritanism" in Catholic moral theology.[4]

I have no wish to pass judgment here on the—to my mind—quite justifiable attempt to construct a theological ethic. I hope merely to draw attention to the optimistic and rather too straight-forward character of many of these attempts in order to bring out clearly the changed climate of opinion prevailing even in Catholic ethics, now that, both in doctrine and in practice, Christ's place in ethics has become a real problem for many. I shall therefore formulate certain constantly heard questions: What is Christ's real significance as the author of salvation in ordering one's existence in the world? How far can Christian law, as handed down in an ecclesiastical tradition, be taken as an intrinsic norm in deciding how one should live in the world? Of what use is the Gospel in resolving such complicated and "secular" questions as the problem of war and peace, the race problem and the popula-tion question?

The novelty does not lie in the questions, but rather in the

Moral Theology I (Westminster, 1958), pp. 60-103; J. Walgrave, "Standpunten en stromingen in de huidige moraaltheologie," in *Tijdschrift voor theologie* I (1961), pp. 48-79 (with French summary).

[4] L. Buys, "Onze moraaltheologie en de bergrede," in *Opstellen aangeboden aan Mgr. van Noort* (Utrecht, 1946), pp. 34-59; Latin translation of this paper in *Studia Moralia* II (Academia Alfonsiana, Institutum theologiae moralis) (Rome, 1964), pp. 11-41.

growing impatience with a too facile recourse to the Gospel, the Sermon on the Mount, brotherly love—in short, a recourse to faith and the scriptures for answers. These questions might not have been so sharply delineated had not the Christian awakening been so deliberately and so vehemently proclaimed in post-war moral theology. It might be said that what was then passed on to ethics as a liberating *message* is now receiving a second and more critical examination. Despite the change in mentality, it would still be possible to speak of a direct and continuous development.

And yet it seems that we are dealing here with a real shift in attitude and in the problems engaging post-war moral theology, a shift occasioned by the almost violent confrontation with the problem of secularism, although the word itself is comparatively new. This secularism has revealed itself within or to Catholic moral theology in the form of three occurrences or, more accurately perhaps, phenomena: situational ethics, the world problems of war and population policies (including birth control), and the relationship of Church and world as set out, provisionally at least, in the *Pastoral Constitution on the Church in the Modern World*. I shall try to indicate briefly the unrest to which these phenomena have given rise in the field of moral theology, an unrest that is clearly connected with the problem of secularism.

Situation ethics[5] may of course be viewed as one of many subsidiary questions confronting moral theology. It may also be maintained that the whole problem of situation ethics is mainly a philosophical-ethical question. This, however, would be to treat the question altogether too lightly. The fact alone that situation ethics is still a recurrent and almost obtrusive problem and is

---

[5] We mention here only a few fundamental studies from the Catholic viewpoint for purposes of orientation: J. Fuchs, *Situation und Entscheidung* (Frankfurt a. M., 1952); K. Rahner, "Situationethik und Sündenmystik," in *Stimmen der Zeit* 145 (1949-1950), pp. 330-42; *idem*, "Uber die Frage einer formalen Existentialethik," in *Schriften zur Theologie* II (Einsiedeln, 1955), pp. 227-46; *idem*, "Zur situationsethik aus ökumenischer sicht," in *Schriften zur Theologie* VI (Einsiedeln, 1965), pp. 537-54; J. Ford and G. Kelly, *Contemporary Moral Theology* I (Westminster, 1958), pp. 104-40.

once again attracting attention in the context of secular ethics
(cf. for example, John A. T. Robinson and J. Fletcher[6]) is, to
say the least, significant. If, leaving all incidental matters aside,
we state the essential problem of situation ethics as: "How can
I know God's will in this world?", then we are immediately faced
with certain categories which Catholic moral theologians have
also debated, without as yet arriving at any solution. These
categories form aspects of the problem of secularism considered
from the viewpoint of the believer. Situation ethics is concerned
with God's presence in Jesus Christ in the world today and with
the essential character of the guidance of the Spirit; it is preoccupied with the historicity of human existence and consequently with the significance of an evangelical morality in the
face of a totally changed world situation.

The fluidity and complexity of the nature of the modern world
and man's coming of age in the face of the powers and forces of
a "higher order" are contrasted with the radicalism and the
authority of an evangelical and ecclesiastical moral message. The
possibility of living a holy life in a sinful world is at stake and
with it the meaning of the power of grace, even in fringe situations and despite human compromise. Within the ethics not only
of the Reformed Churches, but also of the Catholic Church,
situation ethics poses theological problems, all closely linked
with the faith situation of the Christian in the world.[7]

The problems of war and population have brought about a
confrontation between ethics and secularism in a very special
way. Here, too, the chief concern is not merely the solution of
intrinsic questions, but the problem of how to approach them.
No one, naturally enough, expects the Gospel to provide concrete directives for politicians or planners,[8] yet, with this reserva-

---

[6] J. Fletcher, *Situation Ethics. The New Morality* (Philadelphia) (the
Anglican viewpoint).
[7] Cf. J. Metz, "Weltverständnis im Glauben," in *Geist und Leben* 35
(1962), pp. 165-84.
[8] Cf. K. Rahner, "Grenzen der Amtskirche," in *Schriften zur Theologie*
VI (Einsiedeln, 1965), pp. 499-536; Dutch translation published in
brochure form by P. Brand (Hilversum, 1964) under the title *Grenzen
van de kerk.*

tion, many still continue in doubt as to how far and in what manner the believer can attain salvation in domains in which the world evidently goes its own way.

When we see the Christian Churches struggling to provide at least a ray of light in this obscurity, we realize more clearly that perhaps for the first time the question has been clearly put: How and from what sources must the Church gain her knowledge of the form the world must take, if, at the very least, she is not to derogate from the kingdom of God? The doubt expressed concerning the Church's right to pronounce on matters of morality in marriage is but one symptom of a deeper-lying uncertainty regarding the link between an independent world having its own authoritative bodies and self-evident values and aims, and a salvation which must, after all, be gained in and not outside this world.

From this concrete complex of questions emerges more clearly than ever the difficulty of bridging the gulf between faith and world. This constitutes the essence of the present-day question of secularism as a theological problem. Must we, for example, strip the ethics of war of any theological presuppositions,[9] secularizing it in order to find an adequate and pertinent solution? To give another example, is God's revelation so close to the world and so clear that it is capable of shedding light upon the earthly reality of marriage and birth control? These questions are all concerned with the believer's outlook on the world, and thus at the same time with the theological constitution of Christian ethics.

The problem of the relationship between Church and world has long been a venerable part of tradition as a theological theory, but has now evidently become a burning question within the framework of Catholic theology. Much was written about the Christian's universal responsibility just before and shortly after World War II,[10] but then the Church's approach was that of an

[9] From a suggestion by J. Arntz, "Bijbel, vrede, oorlog," in *Wijsgerig perspectief op maatschappij en wetenschap* 4 (1964), pp. 16-29, esp. pp. 27-9.

[10] For a critical bibliography, see A. van Rijen, "De Zin van het christelijk leven in de wereld," in *Katholiek Archief* 12 (1957), pp. 265-352.

institution both theologically and religiously in control. The way from the Church to the world was clear, and the object was to render the Christian ethically aware of a plain task. Since then, however, a shift has occurred which may be clearly discerned in the *Constitution on the Church in the Modern World*.[11] The world's distinctive position is recognized and faith is once again viewed as faith, nourished on the one hand by the unseen, while on the other hand moving amid the tangible and self-evident values of a world which—and this is perhaps more sharply realized than ever—truly possesses its own meaning, with distinctive norms and values. It would appear that we have lost a simple and lucid harmony between faith (salvation) and world. It has been replaced by a consciousness of a tension between the two which is not solely ascetic and cannot be simply translated into terms of sin and human disbelief. As we shall see, all this may be summed up in the forbidding word "secularism".

Present-day ethics certainly cannot be reproached for not paying heed to our modern world—one has only to consider the publications dealing with work and technique—yet here again we are not solely dealing with a confrontation with new, intrinsic problems. These questions involve the very structure of Christian life in the world. Added to this, it would not be too much to say that at the present time Christian ethics still feels helpless to deal with this world. The world has emerged inevitably as an undercurrent to many concrete problems, and this has rippled the surface of Christian ethics.[12] In the course of this article we shall attempt to illustrate this confrontation between the world and Christian ethics.

II

THEONOMY VERSUS HETERONOMY

John A. T. Robinson, more than other "radical" theologians, is concerned with the ethical aspect of secular theology. It might

[11] Cf. A van Rijen, "De christen in de wereld," in *Tijdschrift voor theologie* 6 (1966), pp. 318-33 (with English summary).

[12] One has only to think of the intensity with which the problem of the world is studied by modern Catholic theology in various publications.

even be said that his pastoral involvement has rendered him more sensitive to the practical problems of life than to dogmatic theories. It has indeed been rightly suggested that his famous book *Honest to God* [13] should be read from back to front, beginning with the chapter "The New Morality".[14] In the remaining chapters he attempts to bolster up his Christian situation ethics with dogmatic theories. In Robinson one may not speak of the absence of God, or of the death of God, but rather of the rejection of a supranaturalistic image of God: a God "up there" and a God "out there". The discussion to which Robinson's work has given rise has made it clear, however, that he is concerned not solely with images and words, but also with the possibility or impossibility of a relationship with God.[15] Our interest lies in the consequences of a changed image of God for Christian ethics. Robinson dismisses the idea of a supranaturalistic ethic in which good and evil are laid down in laws and commandments derived from God. Such a point of view imparts an absolute quality to ethic norms, whereby certain things are always wrong and always sinful.[16]

Beneath the veil of various empiric relationships within the world (for instance, the concrete relations between married couples) lies a hidden world of so-called absolute realities which persist even though the empiric relationships have lost their mundane value and meaning. Marriage, for instance, remains indissoluble, even though the relationship between the partners has become distorted and meaningless from a human point of view. According to Robinson this concept confuses two ways of

[13] J. Robinson, *Honest to God* (London, 1963). This book has been translated into numerous languages. From now on we will quote as far as possible from the original editions of the various works. We only quote from translations when the original is not available.

[14] J. Robinson, *op. cit.*, pp. 112-28. We also quote the Dutch translation of this book, *Eerlijk voor God* (Amsterdam, 1964); cf. J. Hoekendijk, "Kleine Robinsonade, 1963," in *Wending* 18 (1963).

[15] Cf. E. Schillebeeckx, "Evangelische Zuiverheid en menselijke waarachtigheid," in *Tijdschrift voor theologie* 3 (1963), pp. 283-326 (with English summary); *idem*, "Herinterpretatie van het geloof in het licht van de seculariteit," in *Tijdschrift voor theologie* 4 (1964), pp. 109-50.

[16] Robinson, *op. cit*, pp. 113-4.

thought: a species of metaphysics, dating from a pre-scientific period, and a theology that aspires to establish an immediate link between God's will and the fluctuating values and behavior patterns of man in the world.[17] This leads traditional ethics to a legalistic interpretation of the Sermon on the Mount which distorts its parabolic and prophetic character.

Robinson calls this kind of ethics "heteronomous" since it derives its norm from "out there". Its strength lies in its emphasis on absolute, objective moral values, which excludes any relativism within the ethic. Its weakness, however, is that it must seek the basis for the validity of its norms not in reality and in actual situations, but in a God who is no longer believed in.[18]

This rejection of a heteronomous ethic does not imply for Robinson a lapse into an autonomous morality à la Kant. A third possibility exists—that of a theonomous ethic in which the transcendent is situated not outside man, but in the concrete relationship between people. In the depth of the unique relationship between people, which must be judged on its own meaning and value, man finds those consecrated, sacred and absolutely unconditional principles which he must obey. "For the Christian this means that he recognizes the unconditional love of Jesus Christ, the man for others, as the ultimate basis of his existence, and as the basis of every relationship and every decision." [19] There is in consequence but one absolute norm: love. Nothing is prescribed but love, which must find its own form and determination in each situation, without recourse to material absolute norms.

In a later work, *Christian Morals Today*,[20] Robinson has attempted a closer definition of this situation ethic. He also defends it against the reproach of relativism and libertinism. This series of articles reveals the essentially practical and pastoral character of Robinson's entire theory. He attempts to define this ethic in

[17] *Ibid.*, pp. 115-6.
[18] *Ibid.*, pp. 117-20. Parallel ideas may be found in J. Fletcher, *op. cit.*, *passim*.
[19] J. Robinson, *op. cit.*, p. 121.
[20] J. Robinson, *Christian Morals Today* (London, 1964); Dutch translation: *Verschuiving in de moraal* (Amsterdam, 1965).

three polarities: fixity and freedom, law and love, authority and experience. He tries to give due value to the emphasis placed by traditional ethics upon the first term of each pair of concepts, while at the same time giving them a fresh interpretation. Fixity, law and authority do not refer to a sort of absolute content of the norms, but to the intention, the aim behind them, which is love.

Many have been disappointed that, after his weighty and ostensibly revolutionary beginnings, Robinson arrives at a situation ethic which cannot even be considered as a new variant of long-existing forms. It is also clear that Robinson is swayed by certain philosophical misconceptions and biases which may even prevail over the theological basis of his arguments. Nonetheless, we are convinced that Robinson has posed for traditional Christian ethics (and this includes Catholic moral theology) some very pertinent and, in fact, theological questions which are nonetheless valid for being phrased in unfortunate and somewhat shallow terms.

Robinson has already raised the question (which will constantly recur): What assistance does the will of God offer me in my ethical dealings in the world? Relationship to God's will becomes problematic in ethics, and consequently so does association with God in worldly activities. Robinson's answer to this question is love for one's fellowmen, but one must not forget that this, for him, is an answer of faith.[21] Belief in Jesus Christ introduces love to the world and with it relationship to God. This, however, does not immediately solve for Robinson the intrinsic problem of ethics, for love provides no ready-made norms; the content of the action must really be deduced from "experience", from the empiric reality of the actual relationships within the world, even though love provides a guideline, a perspective.

Robinson introduces the theme of man's own coming of age. He must seek his own way in the world, "believing" all the while that he is close to God. The rejection of a heteronomous ethic does not imply for Robinson the rejection of God. It does mean, however, that God's presence cannot be taken for granted, nor

[21] J. Robinson, *Honest to God,* pp. 122-8.

can there be an automatic appeal to his will from the particular life situations.

That this search for the *meaning* of these categories—will of God and law of God—evidently constitutes a very real problem which preoccupies modern man, and that, in the search, a certain tendency toward "secularization" occurs even outside theology, may be illustrated by the thesis of Ricoeur, who thinks that one must speak of a "demythologization" of current religious ideas in ethics.[22]

In Ricoeur's view one should render unto ethics those things that are ethical and not attempt to project ethical values onto heaven. If a link must be established between religion and ethics, then it should not be via the concept of a so-called law or will of God[23] which is intended to form, as it were, the basis of the ethic. The will of God (and this means his plan of salvation) echoes merely along the fringes of ethics as a message, as *kerygma,* which refers not to a mythical beginning of a command of creation originally given by God, but to the historical fact of election in Jesus Christ. Only through a *kerygma,* and thus via faith, does the ethics of worldly relationships come into contact with God; a secular charge is reinterpreted as salvation.

Ricoeur's idea, rendered here only summarily and incompletely, contains echoes of the reformatory theme of law and grace, but it is noteworthy that parallel ideas can also be detected in contemporary Catholic thinking. When Arntz[24] (and also, to a certain extent, Kwant[25]) pleads for a detheologizing of ethical secular problems (the question of war and peace, for example), he means not only that historical revelation provides no arguments or norms for a particular mode of behavior or for human decisions, but also, in principle, that in the matter of ethics man

[22] Paul Ricoeur, "Démythiser l'accusation," in *Démythisation et morale* (Astes du Colloque, Rome, January 7-12, 1965) (Aubier), pp. 48-65.

[23] *Ibid.,* pp. 55-56.

[24] Cf. J. Arntz, "De betekenis van de theologie voor een strategie van de vrede," in *Annalen van het Thijngenootschap* 54 (1966), pp. 155-186 (with German summary).

[25] R. Kwant, "Gods liefde en medemenselijkheid," in *Tijdschrift voor theologie* 3 (1963).

can and may only be referred to the world, shared by believer and unbeliever alike.

God does not directly or obviously intervene in any ethical solution. Faith (and thus theology) moves on a different plane, that of the ultimate meaning of life, which neither directly motivates nor normatively clarifies human behavior.

One of the chief trends or characteristics of secularization now comes more sharply into focus. God's involvement in ethical acts is no longer clear or self-evident to modern man when viewed from the world: ethically, the world is self-contained. Faith alone can establish a relationship between God and ethics, but this relationship then exists more on the level of a reinterpretation of life as salvation than on that of new motives or different norms.

III

ETHICS FOR A WORLD COME OF AGE

I have considered Robinson first, since he synthesized a long-existing trend, rendering it accessible to many and thus strengthening and intensifying the movement of secular theology. We now return to the figure of Bonhoeffer, virtually the originator of secular theology as it has developed in recent years, even though he was preceded by theologians of such stature as Tillich, Bultmann, Ebeling and Fuchs.

In the field of Christian secular ethics, Bonhoeffer is a central figure. Indeed, he is essentially an ethical writer. He has a considerable ethical *oeuvre* to his credit, but I shall confine myself here to indicating certain themes which only emerge clearly in his last letters from prison,[26] although it is possible to trace in them

[26] Dietrich Bonhoeffer, *Widerstand und Ergebung* (Briefe und Aufzeietnungen aus der Haft) (Munich, 1951). We quote from the edition of Siebenstern Taschenbuch Verlag (Münster/Hamburg, ⁸1966). A Dutch translation appeared under the title *Verzet en Overgave* (Amsterdam, 1966). The most important letters for our subject are those of April 30, 1944, May 5, 1944, May 25, 1944, June 8, 1944, June 27, 1944, July 8, 1944, July 16, 1944, July 18, 1944 and August 3, 1944. The most important literature on Bonhoeffer may be found in four collections: *Die*

links with his earlier works. In brief notes, sometimes vague and enigmatic, but always stimulating, he outlined a vision which vividly states the problem of a secular Christian ethic. This vision has been taken up and variously interpreted by later authors.

Bonhoeffer's basic theme in the *Letters from Prison* is man come of age, who is at the same time a secular person. Several associated motives and characteristics are involved in this idea of man come of age. In the first place he is an a-religious person who has discovered that he does not need God as a so-called transcendent solution to the various needs or perplexities of life. Modern man has rightly rejected the *deus ex machina* of religion who provided a refuge beyond and above the world for all human defects and deficiencies.

This rejection of a God beyond or above the world also implies, however, the abandoning of a kind of supraterrestrial salvation, to be achieved in a sort of spiritual inner life or in some hereafter. These religious concepts of God and salvation are foreign to the Gospel. The Gospel shows us a God "central to our lives and yet beyond it"; the important thing here is not the "beyond" but the world. "That which is beyond the world asserts itself through the Gospel as of the world." [27] The Gospel therefore brings us a "salvation through history" from which a flight into the eternal is not possible. "Life on earth should not be set aside before its time." [28]

Salvation in the world, on this side of eternity, is a secular process. This also means that the Gospel is addressed to man in his entirety: not only in his needs (as so often in traditional Christianity) but also in his grandeur, in his joy, in his worldly attainments. The Gospel thus allows the world to exist in its secular character and directs man to live a secular life.

What, however, is the factual and thus the ethical significance of this secularism, this temporal quality, this maturity in evan-

---

mündige Welt (Munich, 1955-1963). The Dutch reader will find a good introduction to Bonhoeffer in J. Sperna Weiland's *Orientatie, Nieuwe wegen in de theologie* (Baarn, 1966), pp. 80-93.

[27] Letter of August 5, 1944: *Widerstand und Ergebung*, p. 137.

[28] Letter of June 27, 1944: *op. cit.*, p. 166.

gelical faith? It is only possible to deduce what Bonhoeffer had in mind from a number of unconnected texts. One might attempt to resume his argument thus: in this world the believer must devote himself entirely to his worldly task, without any expectation of being sustained by an almighty, helping, intervening God. He may, however, at the same time *believe* that this secular activity brings God into this world. But this present God is a powerless and suffering God, and as such he is with us and helps us.[29]

This idea of a suffering God emerges as an unexpected theme which is not elaborated; it might be translated as an absence of God, a life in the presence of a God who remains invisible, nowhere making his presence felt, and to whom man can cling only in faith. One fact which does emerge is that for Bonhoeffer only one Christian possibility exists of approaching God or of gaining salvation: to devote oneself unreservedly to the task in the world.

Only toward the end and without any preparation does the more concrete theme emerge which recurs so often among later authors: the only way to meet God is through a meeting with one's neighbor and through selfless devotion to him.[30] As Bonhoeffer saw them, faith and salvation may thus be called secular and temporal, since they can only be attained in the world, in secular relationships and forms. Bonhoeffer therefore considered it as one of the tasks of a modern theology to reinterpret all the fundamental categories of the Gospel (salvation, sin, penance, prayer) in a non-religious manner. This task he did not live long enough to carry out himself.[31]

Bonhoeffer's ideas may be said to contain something of a contradiction. On the one hand he pleads for the evangelical recognition of man's magnificent potential, while on the other he stresses man's participation in God's powerlessness in this world. In his *Ethics,* accountability was already the fundamental cate-

[29] *Op. cit.,* pp. 178 and 183.
[30] *Op. cit.,* p. 191.
[31] Cf. G. Ebeling, "Die nicht-religiöse Interpretation Biblischer Begriffe," in *Die mündige Welt* II (Munich, 1956), pp. 12-73.

gory of his ethical theory. This is now complicated by the theme of God's absence. The simplest (since it is the most straight-forward) interpretation of Bonhoeffer's enigmatic phrase, "to live in the world *quasi Deus non daretur"*, might be that it is precisely a faith as referring to the Unseen that gives the believer the courage, but also the painful duty, to seek his own way in the "absent nearness" of God, which is all that he can hold to.

Bonhoeffer did not elaborate his vision into a coherent system of ethics; he left us only an outline. However, the spirit, the mentality, behind such a Christian ethic is clearly defined, and is taken up by later writers. It consists in a qualified identifica-tion of salvation and world structure, an historification and secu-larization of the way toward ultimate salvation, and a summons (optimistic) to tackle the problems of life and of the world with nothing but human resources. It is, in fact, precisely the believer who will hear this summons and have the courage to carry it out in painful awareness of the absence of God. It is clear that any further interpretation can diverge into two extremes, as we shall later see: either faith is reduced to ethics (van Buren), which implies a total and radical ethicizing of faith, or an almost tragic fideism develops which is secular while hoping against hope for God's blessing.

In my opinion this latter position is to a certain extent adopted by a German theologian, Dorothee Sölle, in her book *Representa-tion. A Chapter of Theology Following the "Death of God"*.[32] Although she dissociates herself from Bonhoeffer, she has devel-oped a certain interpretation of his basic theme. This theologian is more obsessed by God's absence than by his "death". God is not clearly present; evidently he never helps, never intervenes. Man is thrown back upon himself. He must find his own solution to life's problems.

In this situation, which the believer must finally face honestly and courageously, and which implies a real (and not merely

[32] Dorothee Sölle, *Stellvertretung* (Ein Kapittel Theologie nach dem Tode Gottes) (Stuttgart/Berlin, 1965). We could only find the Dutch translation, *Plaatsbekleding* (Een hoofdstuk theologie na de dood van God) (Utrecht). We quote from this translation.

apparent) absence of God, she attempts to interpret Christ's significance as God's representative among men and man's representative with God. Through a laborious philosophical analysis of the phenomenon of representation and an historical outline of the traditional theological interpretations of this function, she finally arrives at the thesis that man, who, being helpless, must always have recourse to representation, finds in Christ someone who will take up his discredited cause. It is he who believes, hopes and loves in our place.

But this representation by Christ is only temporary; man must learn to do his own believing, hoping and loving, for God is concerned with man.[33] The fact that Christ acts as our representative means that he keeps our place open so that we can later occupy it again ourselves. We need Christ so that God may not wash his hands of us.

But the place which we must learn to occupy ourselves is our place in the world. We ought now, in our history and within our world, as sons of God, to bear responsibility for the world. In Christ, the person of God, we are endowed with a freedom that liberates us from all the so-called absolute powers and forces of this world and renders us receptive to this world in an unprejudiced, disinterested and authentic manner.

The believer must therefore learn to live in the world, and once again, in a manner strongly reminiscent of Bonhoeffer, we have the somewhat enigmatic definition of this secular state. Christ entered this life for us, in our place. But we must learn to live ourselves, by not regarding the secular and its associated alienation as something foreign to God, but as a manner of his being with us.[34] Here again we have secularism as a courageous justification in faith of a life that offers no prospects and no solution, which may and must expect no solution from God, but which must in fact *believe* in this tragic lack as a form of God's presence.

What is the meaning of this absence of God? Once again we

---

[33] D. Sölle, *op. cit.*, p. 112.
[34] *Ibid.*, p. 116.

come very close to Bonhoeffer. God has become superfluous as a working hypothesis and can nowhere be recognized as a mighty God. Naive theism is definitely *passé*.[35] This absence must now be accepted as God's being-for-us. In this being-for-us, Christ has an essential function, since he is God's representative among us. For the time being he replaces God; he deputizes for him. Without Christ we would have no reason to await a God who is as yet absent and invisible. In Jesus the possibility of waiting for God has become clear, and this is the significance of his resurrection. Yet Christ's representative role, too, is only temporary. Christ is God's representative but at the same time his precursor.

It is by no means clear who exactly, in Sölle's view, this Christ is. Is he more than a symbol, more than the message as transmitted in the Gospel? [36] This is one of the many points upon which the reader remains unenlightened. But two things do emerge clearly in Sölle. No other way of faith remains to us than to accept total responsibility for the world, without looking for any other presence of God than that of his powerlessness and his weakness. Man must have the courage to accept total secularism. On the other hand, the hope remains that in this state God will ultimately come to us (from a future) and this hope (both from our side and from God's) is Christ.

Once again the autonomy of ethics as a secular mandate clearly emerges. One can sense something of the writer's intention if one looks about, as a believer, and dares honestly to admit how we really live: doing what has to be done without ever perceiving any indication of a God who in any way intervenes in the world.

But is there not a danger of departing from any Christian tradition in creating what is in fact a sort of fideistic parallelism between belief in an absent God and a life in the world, without being able to indicate any point of contact? Would it not be more consistent (but this, too, would signify a departure from a Christian ethic) simply to identify salvation and world—as do

[35] *Ibid.*, p. 146.
[36] *Ibid.*, pp. 151-2.

the writers mentioned in the following paragraph—reducing salvation to the world? In this way it might be possible to retain
Christ as a sign that hope exists, although it is impossible to
define this hope or trace its basis in any form of reality. Sölle
does draw our attention to the unmistakable fact with which the
believer must come to terms in his ethics: that man, by his own
power and insight and yet before the face of an unseen God, fulfills a routine task in the world. An effortless recourse to automatic grace, miraculous flashes of enlightenment and grace-filled
directives are not so easily reserved for any Christian ethic.
Sölle's question remains urgent: What is the significance of an
appeal to God for an ethic based on faith? It is no longer possible
to avoid the task of showing clearly (theologically, at least)
where God is to be found within a system of ethics. Sölle follows
Bonhoeffer in courageously setting before us the inescapable and
as yet theologically unresolved problem of the faith which
changes everything in the life of the Christian, yet alters nothing
in a way that can be proved or seen.

IV

FAITH REDUCED TO ETHICS

Limiting ourselves to recent forms of secular theology and
thus bypassing certain important figures like Tillich, I shall
group together in this section some extreme manifestations of
secular "Christian" ethics. Despite the differences separating the
ideas of van Buren, Altizer and Hamilton, there remain sufficient
symptomatic and typological similarities to justify discussing them
together.

Van Buren's *The Secular Meaning of the Gospel* [37] is important

[37] Paul van Buren, *The Secular Meaning of the Gospel* (based on an
analysis of its language) (London, 1963). The Dutch translation, *De
seculiere betekenis van het evangelie,* will appear in 1967. A good summary can be found in J. Sperna Weiland, *op. cit.,* pp. 114-20. See also
Th. Ogletree, *The "Death of God" Controversy,* pp. 39-59 (with extremely good critical remarks). The Anglican-Thomist viewpoint is given
by E. Mascall in *The Secularization of Christianity* (London, 1965).

in our context because he draws such radical conclusions from a secular interpretation of faith. For van Buren it is senseless to speak of God from a neo-positivist viewpoint. For this reason he desires to reduce theology at least to christology. He does not wrestle with an absence or lamented "death of God", but in order to justify faith he turns easily and unproblematically to the historically verifiable figure of Christ. Faith for van Buren then becomes a new outlook on life, a fresh perspective, implying an "engagement" and proceeding from a discernment, a new discovery drawn from the story of Jesus.[38]

It is not made clear what gives rise to this "faith" (it had its origin in the significance of the events of Easter for the disciples), but van Buren attempts a "secular" interpretation of its content, in this case adapted to the empiric mentality of modern man whose chief concern is a modern way of life and the value he attaches to human relationships. Through Jesus, who can be known as a historical personage, faith imparts to man a "contagious" freedom which liberates him for his fellowmen.[39]

I shall not for the moment go any deeper into the questions that van Buren's theory immediately provokes from the theological viewpoint, such as: What is Christ's significance as the origin and mediator of freedom without reference to a transcendent God? How must one understand this imparting of freedom without having recourse to the traditional idea of grace? [40]

Of primary importance for us is the fact that van Buren obviously wishes to link his ethics of freedom with the historical person of Jesus and thus continue in a "Christian" tradition. However—and we shall go deeper into this shortly—the question is whether Christ does not function here solely as a model, an example, with no claim to any uniqueness at all, let alone the right to be considered as a *causa salutis*.

[38] P. van Buren, *op. cit.*, p. 132.
[39] *Ibid.*, pp. 141ff.
[40] See the criticism of Th. Ogletree, *op. cit.* Cf. H. Kuitert, *De realiteit van het geloof* (Kampen, 1966), pp. 143-4, for the anti-metaphysical trend in modern theological development.

Even more important, the efficacy (and in fact the content) of faith is transferred to ethics. Faith is accomplished in freedom, which is then viewed as a disinterested devotion to one's neighbor. This love in freedom is then no longer in any way a means of finding God, as in Robinson, Bonhoeffer and Sölle; it is confined within the limits of the world and reduced to pure and simple ethics. Faith is ethicized and thus radically horizontalized. In the authors already discussed, something (in some cases a great deal) still remained of the essential scriptural drama between God and man; here faith is reduced to man's struggle against the powers that threaten his freedom.[41] From the theological viewpoint this is the acme of secularization, the reduction of faith to a purely worldly mandate lacking any transcendent or eschatological perspective, whereby the story of Jesus is told as a *cantus firmus*.

The striking point is that, while van Buren in fact lays the entire accent of his christology upon an ethic of Jesus, this ethic appears to consist in the reiteration of a vague concept of freedom. It is thus impossible for us to develop further in his own terms the ethical consequences of his theory in this sense.

We would do well, however, to ponder the significance of such a reduction of faith to ethics for this ethic itself. We are immediately struck by the burden which this would impose upon a Christian ethic. The radically disinterested existing-for-others must now all at once be taken as a self-evident and profound reality (evidently comprised in human experience) replacing the reality of grace and a relationship with God, as though the depth and grandeur of ethical man were so self-evident and "empirically obvious" in our world!

The reduction of faith to ethics threatens to produce an elite Christianity. Whether this elite coincides with the secular man who is the object of van Buren's theory is doubtful, to say the least. Van Buren thinks he has found in ethics a demonstrable reality capable of being experienced in this world; nevertheless, his entire ethic is linked with Jesus, for it is based upon a free-

---

[41] Cf. H. Kuitert, *op. cit.*, pp. 145-6.

dom transferred from him to us. This relationship with Jesus remains in van Buren a mysterious reality which he rather assumes than proves. This lends an unreal and somewhat arbitrary note to his option for a Christian morality intended to take the place of faith.[42]

The theories of the "death-of-God" theologians, Hamilton and Altizer, are of a completely different stamp. They do, however, have one point in common with van Buren: they reduce theology (faith) to a system of ethics. With these two authors we have reached the end of the road leading away from traditional theology. They are no longer concerned with an obsolescent image of God, with the absence of God (Bonhoeffer, Sölle) or with an unknowable God (van Buren). They go so far as to deny the God of Christianity. For both these writers it is impossible to reconcile the existence of God with the maturity and independence of man in the world.[43]

For Hamilton this denial of God results in a positive turning toward the world. This he considers to be in the spirit of the Reformation which initiated the movement from the cloister to the world.[44] What still appeals to him in the Christian tradition is its involvement in the human struggle for human dignity and justice in the world. With enviable optimism, found later in Harvey Cox, he enlarges upon the possibility of man's reforming the world. Secularization for him is in no way a threat to modern man, but offers instead a possibility to intensify authentic human values.

But this turning toward the world is also linked for Hamilton with the figure of Christ. Jesus for him is a "place to be", a standpoint from which man can turn in a disinterested manner to his

[42] Cf. H. Kuitert, *op. cit.*, p. 143.
[43] For a fundamental criticism of the German use of the concept of religion and the conclusions drawn concerning an "intervening" God as typical of a religious form of faith, see A. Richardson, *Religion in Contemporary Debate* (London, 1966), pp. 17-29.
[44] W. Hamilton, *The New Essence of Christianity* (New York and London, 1961). After reading the original we have made grateful use of the excellent critical summary of Th. Ogletree, *The "Death of God" Controversy* (London, 1966), pp. 26-38.

neighbor. The Christian's task is "to become Jesus", which means to identify himself with the needs and requirements of his neighbor. He desires to draw up an imitation of Christ, but has not yet developed this theory further.[45]

Altizer[46] feels even more strongly than Hamilton that no theology can ignore the fact of our modern profane culture and, in the absence of any religious feeling in modern man, must seek a profane form of Christianity. For Altizer this profane form of Christian faith is represented by the great figures of modern times who, in the crisis of a changed age, have attempted to rediscover Christ's presence in the world.

Among these great figures he includes Freud, Nietzsche and Hegel. In addition, Altizer has attempted, by comparing Eastern mysticism and Christianity, to throw some light upon the true nature of Christian faith. His basic theory is built up gradually around the theme of the incarnation of the Word; the essence of the Christian faith is a movement of the sacred toward the profane, not in order to deny or replace the profane, but rather to be completely incarnated in it. There is no question of a participation in or a return to an original divine reality, but rather of a journey through the movement of history toward the end. Time, history, and the world are for Altizer the only places where the sacred is to be found. This entry of the sacred into the profane means, however, that God has, and must have, abdicated as eternal and pure Being in order to enter into the process of this world, and has thus assumed the transient, changeable, adaptable nature of this world. The transcendent God has thus become a God immanent in this world, and this signifies his death. Jesus Christ is this God who empties himself of his Godhead. God does not exist outside the person of Jesus Christ.

[45] Cf. Th. Ogletree, op. cit., p. 55.

[46] The two most important works by Th. Altizer are *Mircea Eliade and the Dialectic of the Sacred* (Philadelphia, 1963) and *The Gospel of Christian Atheism* (Philadelphia, 1966). Ogletree, op. cit., pp. 60-84, also gives an excellent summary of his ideas. Hamilton and Altizer have collaborated in summarizing their ideas in *Radical Theology and the Death of God* (New York, 1966); Dutch translation: *Radicale Theologie en de Dood van God* (Utrecht, 1966).

This liberation from a distant God, existing outside the world and dominating man, also means that man is made free and independent. The traditional God stood in man's way, and the profane prophets, from whom Altizer derives his inspiration, have made a courageous attempt to free themselves from this God. But the question remains: For what purpose has man been set free? The task in the world must be for Altizer truly a presence of Jesus, and he now finds this presence in Nietzsche's idea of the eternal recurrence.[47]

This, however, does not mean that man simply allows himself to be plunged into an eternal senseless circle of an ever recurring world process. It means that he (with Nietzsche) actively desires this eternal recurrence, or, in other words, that he welcomes every moment, concrete, meaningless and impenetrable though it may be. The Christian task is never to flee that moment, seeking the consolation of eternity or of a divine plan, but courageously to live this life as it is. In this way the sacred is revealed in the profane. In Altizer's words, "to confess Jesus means to turn to the world, to the heart of the profane, acknowledging that Christ is present here and nowhere else. If we are prepared to confess that Christ is fully present only in the moment that lies before us, we can in truth love the world, embracing its pain and darkness as an epiphany of Christ".[48] In other words, faith is the rejection of any appeal to an eternal superterrestrial God and the welcoming of a Christ in the midst of the changeable, contingent world.

It is clear from the foregoing that with Altizer we have abandoned not only traditional theology but also sober thought. This is a mystic speaking, a poet who scarcely attempts to construct a logical synthesis from his criticism of traditional Christianity. In one aspect, however, Altizer is an important figure in relation to secular ethics. In Bonhoeffer and Sölle we have already encountered a strange sort of mysticism, a turning toward

---

[47] Th. Altizer, *The Gospel of Christian Atheism*, pp. 147-57.
[48] *Ibid.*, pp. 155-6 (quoted in Ogletree, *op. cit.*, p. 77).

the world in (the form of) a kind of *compassio*. God's absence is the presence of a suffering, abdicating God with whom the Christian can show solidarity in his compassion for the world. The cross of Christ in Bonhoeffer and Sölle and the *kenosis* of God in Jesus are classical evangelical themes which are here taken up and reinterpreted, since man—and this is important— feels impelled in a Christian manner to accept the world as it is. Faith is not taking refuge in the consolation of an "upper world", but consists in enduring this world.

In Bonhoeffer and Sölle, however, this does not mean a passive mysticism of acceptance of the world, although this is to some extent true in Altizer. Ogletree, therefore, in his excellent analysis, has felt obliged to utter a warning against a denial of all ethics in the work of Altizer. The idea of an "eternal recurrence", or, in other words, of an identification with the real absurd world, impels Altizer in the direction of "so be it" and consequently toward a form of acceptance of God's will, which is precisely what he felt himself obliged to reject. And yet Ogletree feels that Altizer's theory is not without points of contact for a system of ethics. It is precisely this total and radical openness to the *praesentia Christi,* Christ present at this moment, which can free man to seek the correct answer and the adequate solution to just this situation, without prejudice and without recourse to any ideology (the ideology of God's will, providence or eternal laws).[49]

It is my opinion, however, that Altizer's search (and this he has in common with Bonhoeffer and Sölle) is leading him in another direction, that of a sort of fideistic endurance of the ills of this world, since for the believer, the unseen is present in what is visible of a world without prospects. It really amounts to this: all attempts to change the world (and no one will deny that this is man's task) must be made without being able to see what they mean for God. Faith, however, gives man the strength to bear this discrepancy between the seen and the unseen.

[49] Th. Ogletree, *op. cit.,* pp. 81-2.

V
SECULARIZATION AS THE TASK OF THE BELIEVER

Thus far we have seen how the crisis of faith surrounding the absence of God in our present-day world results in nearly all secular theologians turning to the world. The world becomes the place where "God" is to be found. In the authors we have looked at so far the problems surrounding the existence of God have formed the point of departure for a secular theology, and their thinking ends in the confirmation of the world.

With the American theologian Harvey Cox, whose stimulating and cleverly-written book *The Secular City*[50] has become a best seller with a far reaching influence, the situation is somewhat different. Only toward the end of his book does he deliberately concern himself with the question of God. His point of departure is really a description of man's situation in the modern world.

This he defines as secularization, and secularization for Cox means in essence the recognition of the intrinsic value of humanity and of the autonomy and accountability of man. He naturally links this situation of man with the problem of faith and religion, but, as Krinkels has, in my opinion, rightly pointed out,[51] it is noteworthy that for Cox secularization is not primarily or solely a characteristic of a believing existence but of human existence *tout court*. According to Cox (who derives his definition from Peursen[52]) secularization is man's liberation from the tutelage of religion and metaphysics, but this at the same time signifies his liberation from every ideology and from every would-be absolute system. In Cox's view this emancipation is an authentic consequence of biblical faith which, especially as

[50] H. Cox, *The Secular City*. A study of secularization and urbanization in theological perspective (London, 1965); Dutch translation: *De Stad van de Mens* (Utrecht, 1966).
[51] M. Krinkels, "Secularisering. Een poging tot begripsverheldering," in *Theologie en Zielzorg* 62 (1966), p. 273.
[52] See footnote 1.

manifested in the Old Testament, implies a desacralization of life in the fields of both politics and ethics.

In this he agrees with Friedrich Gogarten. At the present time this secularization is taking place in the context of the urbanization process which is transforming the world into the secular city, characterized by anonymity and mobility, by pragmatism and profanity.[53] Modern man is not preoccupied by questions concerning an "other" world, but he is fascinated by the concrete world about him which he wishes to reform and improve through pragmatic solutions.

The scope of this article does not allow us to follow in detail Cox's fascinating analysis of the modern approach to life and of the present human situation. The important thing for us is that his thesis results in a particular concept of "theological" ethics, which we shall now attempt to define. For Cox, secularization means not the denial or rejection of a transcendent God, but a reinterpretation of God's relationship to man and vice versa. The biblical God is a God whom we discern in the historical social reality of this world, a God who invites man to a free, self-deciding partnership, a God who offers new possibilities within the history of this world. We discover the action of God in what theologians have called "historical events", but what might be better termed "social change".[54] This theology of "social change" is at the heart of Harvey Cox's thesis and with it he introduces a distinctive form of secular Christian ethics. He defines this theology of social change in the framework of his concept of the task of the Christian Church. We shall, however, postpone our comprehensive description of this function of the Church in secular theology until later.

Characteristic of our time is a rapid social change which, when closely examined, must be called a social revolution. The guidance, orientation and molding of this change in the direction of an improved world is the task of "politics" in the broad sense. The pertinent questions for a present-day theology are:

[53] H. Cox, *op. cit.*, pp. 60-84.
[54] *Ibid.*, p. 105.

What is God's part in this social revolution? Who is really acting in this social revolution, God or man?

For Cox it has become evident in the figure of Jesus that we are here dealing with a partnership between God and man. He finds evidence of this partnership in the structure of each social revolution. On the one hand man finds himself in a particular situation which is, as it were, imposed on him, which is not of his own making, but which on the other hand constitutes a point of departure for his actions. Without going so far as to say that the actual situation is a clear demonstration of God's will, it is nonetheless an indication of the way in which God intends that man should go.[55] The kingdom of God spoken of in the Gospel may perhaps not be identified with the secular city, but our building of human society is in any case our response to the reality of the kingdom of God in our time. The secular city is the kingdom of God in process of realization, although the hope remains that it may grow to an ultimate form which we do not suspect and can only await.[56]

A theology (and an ethic) of social change can find its origin in the analogy which exists between the actual situation of our world and the biblical idea of the kingdom of God. A revolutionary theology must find its point of departure in a gap which exists between the actual situation and a fresh situation which has yet to be thought up and brought about. It so happens that the present secular city presents such a gap, since we realize that our technical resources in various fields have not yet been exploited and utilized in constructive political action.

On the other hand, the Gospel shows us how the God of the scriptures is always a step ahead of man, beseeching him to depart from the country where he lives and to go to the place that he shall point out to him.[57] The actual social situation is a form in which the kingdom summons us to forget what lies behind us and to strive onward to what lies ahead.

[55] *Ibid.*, pp. 111-2.
[56] *Ibid.*, p. 113.
[57] *Ibid.*, p. 116.

This is the essence of what Cox calls "ethical tension" as scripture sees it. The ethical tension seen by the bible is rather different from the tension between what is and what ought to be as usually stated in a philosophical system of ethics. The Gospel does not use a categorical imperative. On the contrary, the Gospel concentrates in the first place upon what is actually occurring and only then issues a summons to a consequent change in attitude and action.[58] In a stimulating but sometimes rather arbitrary-sounding exegesis, Cox now shows that, parallel and analagous to each other in the present world situation and in the scriptures, similar causes are given for man's reluctance to change and a similar catharsis for this reluctance is described. Always and ever it is man's clinging to outmoded forms of thought and life and his lack of courage to accept maturity and responsibility that deter him from revolutionary action. And it is always a social, yet at the same time evangelical, catastrophe (the proclamation of the kingdom of God) which opens man's eyes and summons him to change.

It sometimes seems that the kingdom of God and social catastrophe run parallel in Cox's mind, and sometimes that the world situation is a form of the emerging kingdom. In any case, according to Cox, both point toward a doctrine and an activity which can be summed up as social change. Social change may also be rendered as "secularization", meaning that man lives at the point of intersection between God's activity, as expressed in the influence of history upon man, and man's action upon history in reply. At this point of intersection lies the phenomenon of conversion or, in other words, of responsibility, of the acceptance of adult accountability.[59]

Cox's theory of the Christian's ethical task may be further clarified by his concept of God's "political" activity.[60] For Cox associates God with the idea of "politics" and thinks that,

[58] *Ibid.*
[59] *Ibid.*, pp. 122-3.
[60] *Ibid.*, pp. 248-57.

abandoning mythical and metaphysical discussions on God, there remains the possibility of speaking of God in "political" terms. By politics he understands the complex of activities that form and build up the modern *polis,* the secular city. It will be theology's task to clarify the vital problems of the modern *polis* in the light of the great events in which God acted (the Exodus and Easter) and to provide a new directive. In common with Lehmann,[61] Cox speaks of God's political activity—that is, those actions on God's part which render human life livable. To this corresponds man's political activity, which has the same objectives. We speak of God in a political manner whenever we summon our brother to act responsibly, whenever we cultivate human relationships, whenever we liberate one another from prejudice and immaturity. In all this man confronts God, who truly meets him face to face and who may not be reduced to the world or fellowman. He is, however, a hidden God who only becomes relevant for us in his dealings with and for the world.[62]

In Cox we also find the tendency to translate relationship to God in terms of secular activities, but he is more concerned with social dealings than other writers. Here the building up of the world, salvation and the kingdom of God come so close as to be almost identical, as do theology and ethics.

Against the background of a hidden God who manifests himself only in his political dealings with the world, there emerges a space for revolutionary activity which involves a socially conscious and clearly optimistic ethic. Apart from the question of whether faith, for Cox, does not function merely as the discovery of the secularizing trend of the bible (especially in the Old Testament story of salvation), one may well wonder if he does not display an exaggerated interest in technical, efficient man. There is little room in this ethic for the needs of the individual, and little prospect is held out for the vital questions of suffering, disappointment and death, which even in his city im-

---

[61] P. Lehmann, *Ethics in a Christian Context* (London, 1963), pp. 81-6.
[62] H. Cox, *op. cit.,* pp. 257-68.

pel man back from all technical and social activities to the needs
of his own heart and toward a mode of belief other than "political action".

VI

THE CHURCH'S FUNCTION WITH REGARD TO
A SECULAR CHRISTIAN ETHIC

The secular theologians whom we have already discussed
show a remarkable interest in the meaning, the position and the
function of the Church. Their interest in the place of faith in
the life of the world and their preoccupation with the building
up of this world compel them to define the Church anew as a
"secular body" within this world. It is not our task here to
describe the multiform attempts to arrive at a new ecclesiology.
We are only concerned with the "ethical function" attributed to
the Church. Not surprisingly, perhaps, some theologians consider the Church's significance to be entirely absorbed in and
reduced to her ethical function and task. We shall attempt here
to group together and define the various theories concerning
this aspect of the Church's function.

In a general way one might assert that there is one basic
theme which recurs in various forms in secular theology—
namely, that the Church's function is to serve the world and
its needs. Salvation is promised to the world and must be attained in the world. The Church has absolutely no right to claim
exclusive possession of the reality of salvation.

Without classifying him as a secular theologian, it can still
be said that the theories of Hoekendijk[63] on this point have been
of great significance for this new concept of the Church. Central
figures like Robinson[64] and Harvey Cox[65] expressly refer to
him and claim to develop his ideas. "In the biblical world of the

---

[63] J. Hoekendijk, *De Kerk Binnenste Buiten* (Amsterdam, 1964), pp.
41-55; English translation: *The Church Inside Out* (Philadelphia and
London, 1966).

[64] J. Robinson, *The New Reformation* (London, 1965), p. 72.

[65] H. Cox, *op. cit.*, pp. 144-5; cf. footnote 11 on p. 145.

messianic fulfillment the essential point is the *kingdom* for the *world*. We must hold consistently to this fundamental fact." [66] The kingdom (of God) is involved in the world; it is destined for the world. The essential function of the Church is thus the apostolate—that is, the carrying of the Gospel to the *world*. The Church lives for the world. She can only participate in the Gospel by being willing to serve all. Robinson has similar statements: the house of God is not the Church but the world; the Church is the slave, and the first characteristic of a slave is that he lives in another's house and not in his own; the proper function of the Church is to serve, and this service must be adapted to the needs of the world; the Church's form (and her structure) must thus be adapted to the needs of the world.[67] The Church's service to the world becomes the central concept in attempting to define the Church's place and to describe her function. This service is admittedly viewed in a broader framework of ecclesiastic apostolic activity, for besides service the apostolate also comprises the *kerygma* (the preaching of peace [salvation?]) and *koinonia* (corporate participation in peace).[68] Nonetheless, for secular theology, service remains the clearest, most tangible and most explicit secular function of the Church.

The idea of a "servant Church" can be developed in various directions—theological (as in Hoekendijk) or, more practical, sociological, with particular attention to the structural alterations necessitated by a reformation of the Church as *diakonia*. The main exponents of this theory are Robinson and especially Gibson Winter.[69] Here, however, we wish only to deal with

[66] J. Hoekendijk, *op. cit.*, p. 41.
[67] J. Robinson, *The New Reformation*, pp. 88-100.
[68] J. Hoekendijk, *op. cit.*, p. 50.
[69] G. Winter, *The New Creation as Metropolis* (New York and London, 1963). Drawing his inspiration from Bonhoeffer, Winter sees the Church's task as one of service to man in the struggle against the powers and institutions which frustrate a truly human living together. The Church has fundamentally failed in this task. The prophetic voice of the Church especially will have to point out to man the real problems which demand his attention. The reference is especially to the concrete social problems of our time. Winter, too, is thus preoccupied by the social-ethic function of the Church.

certain statements of Harvey Cox which illustrate the secular interpretation of the Church. He, too, has recourse to Hoekendijk's theory of the triple function of the Church in relation to the world. The Church proclaims (*kerygma*) for the world the end of the powers which menace man's freedom and maturity, but these powers must be interpreted in a concrete secular fashion. As in the Old Testament we are still concerned with a liberation by God from political, cultural and economic "bondage". [70]

Cox immediately transposes the *diakonia* of the Church to the concrete terrain of the secular city. The Church's task there is to heal the fractures to which city life is subject: ethnic and racial tensions, conflict between the have's and the have-not's, competition between political parties, etc.[71]

Finally, the Church must make visible the city of man (*koinonia* as a truly human community) by demonstrating in her own life that it is possible to live together in love despite differences and contrasts.[72] In this manner the Church is God's "avant-garde" (here, too, Cox is inspired by Hoekendijk's ideas and terminology).[73]

It is clear that Cox thinks almost exclusively of the Church as an ethical body within the world, taking "ethical" here in its broadest and highest sense. This emerges even more clearly in his description of the Church as "cultural exorcist".[74] Society is suffering from a sort of communal neurosis expressed in prejudices, rancor, partiality, excessive sensitivity to certain values and blindness to others. According to Cox one may rightly speak of social myths which perpetuate injustice and curtail the freedom to take adequate social action. By analogy with what Jesus did for sick individuals, the Church has here a mission to

[70] H. Cox, *op. cit.*, pp. 127-32.

[71] *Ibid.*, pp. 132-44.

[72] The Church's koinoniac function is to make visible the city of man. Cf. *ibid.*, pp. 144-8.

[73] In the same manner, Cox himself acknowledges Hoekendijk's influence on his ideas on the Church. Cf. *ibid.*, p. 144.

[74] *Ibid.*, pp. 149-63.

exorcise and desacralize social myths and expose their fallaciousness.

Once again one sees (and Cox is here a symptom) how the Church's intervention for good is immediately applied to concrete matters, but in one special direction: that of the social-cultural problems of our world. It must, however, be clearly borne in mind that for Cox, as for Robinson and certainly for Hoekendijk and Winter, the Church as ethical body remains the Church, since in her an *ex parte Dei* filters through into this world. But with Cox this activity on God's part is only positive when it involves a transformation of the world whereby man acts as God's partner or—to use the scriptural images which he likes to employ for mature, secular man—as God's "son" and "steward". This is clearly a serious and believing attempt to define the position of the Church in the modern world.

The work of Paul Lehmann, *Ethics in a Christian Context*,[75] gives an indication of the profound "ecclesiastical ethics" which may evolve from Cox's mode of thought. This book precedes the secular theology proper, but its inspiration is the same. For Lehmann the Church is an ethical reality—that is, a community (*koinonia*) in which man can mature through God's grace. This involves the freedom to be oneself as a man in community with others. The Christian Church (*koinonia*) is the foretaste and sign in the world that God has always acted and continues to act in such a way that human life may be and remain human.[76]

We already find the germ of this idea of the "servant" Church in Bonhoeffer, for whom the most characteristic mark of the Church is her "being for others". The Church does not wish to rule like any other authority, but, like Jesus, she desires con-

---

[75] London, 1963. Several of Lehmann's ideas (the political activity of God) have influenced Cox. From a Catholic standpoint there is certainly criticism to be made of Lehmann's contextual ethics. He arrives ultimately at an ethic of situation which raises various questions. See the witty criticism of Lehmann and of contextual ethics as a whole, especially in an American setting, by J. Gustafson, "Context Versus Principles, A Misplaced Debate in Christian Ethics," in *New Theology* 3, edited by Martin E. Marty and Dean G. Peerman (New York and London, 1966).

[76] Lehmann, *op. cit.*, p. 101.

stantly to lose herself in and for the world.[77] Bonhoeffer had already dealt in detail with the relationship between Church and world in his *Ethics*,[78] but it is only in his *Letters from Prison* that he discovers a Church which exists radically for the world. Her task is simply to tell the world what life in Christ is, while setting the example of "being for others".[79] One question, however, proves a stumbling block: if one accepts the coming of age of the world and, on principle, accepts the world in its worldliness, where then is the Church's area of activity? He was not given time to find an answer.

From the outline of Dorothee Sölle's "theology", given above, it may be deduced that for her the Church's function is limited to representation. The Church is the group of believers which is answerable for someone to God. She vouches for the world before God. She gives God courage to continue waiting for this world. The Church is a *function of the world*. The Church is always present when acting as the world's defender. She knows her clients' interests and advances them with God. She retires into the background whenever the world is capable of fulfilling its own tasks, but is always ready to intervene whenever the world needs her.[80] This Church can also function anonymously, for wherever true humanity is attained, one has representation, and thus Christianity and Church. The institutional Church has the task of developing consciousness which explains and justifies what is truly present elsewhere.[81]

From this brief recapitulation of Sölle's propositions, one may well conclude that for her, too, the function of the Church is above all ethical, the building up of the world. Yet while she retains a background of faith, it does not function clearly as the origin and content of this ethic. In the absence of a God the

---

[77] D. Bonhoeffer, *Widerstand und Ergebung*, p. 193.

[78] D. Bonhoeffer, *Ethik* (Zusammerigestelt und herausgegben von Eberhard Bethge) (Munich, 1963), *passim*, esp. pp. 59-63.

[79] D. Bonhoeffer, *Widerstand und Ergebung*, p. 163 (letter of June 8, 1944).

[80] D. Sölle, *Plaatsbekleding*, pp. 123-4.

[81] *Ibid.*, pp. 151-2.

Church has no option but to assume a secular task, for she is not granted an immediate relationship with God. It does not emerge very clearly from Sölle's work what form of ethics she evolves from her concept of the Church and her interpretation of faith. It will probably be an ethic of common humanity, its content to be further defined by the world itself.

The word "Church" does not occur in the index of van Buren's book, and indeed it occupies but little space in his theological theory. Nonetheless he does devote a short paragraph to "the Church, her actions and words".[82] The Church is for him a somewhat mysterious yet translucent historical reality made up of people who share in the freedom with which they were "infected" through Jesus and who are aware of the source of this freedom. Freedom is again the almost monotonous concept which is also used to define the Church. The Church will continue to communicate and reiterate that particular view of life derived from the historical Gospel.

The Church, however, also has a pronounced ethical function insofar as she summons and admonishes in her preaching. What, however, is the significance of the Church's ethical appeal? For van Buren it is senseless to seek to characterize the Church's ethical exhortations by referring to God's will as the origin of the ethical obligation. In the Church's preaching, reference to God's will means a reference to the story of Jesus, to the events of Easter and to the view of life to which they gave rise. The Church does nothing other than to point out the logical consequences of a particular mode of behavior which follows from the Christian view of life. To say "because it is God's will" is no explanation of the motive for a particular course of action, but a reference to the historical perspective which functions as the context for a particular action.[83]

There may well be then, according to van Buren, a better formula than the "will of God" to indicate what the Church really means and does. All typically "ecclesiastical acts", such

[82] P. van Buren, *The Secular Meaning of the Gospel*, pp. 183-92.
[83] *Ibid.*, pp. 186-7.

as the celebration of the eucharist, prayer and evangelization, are reinterpreted as phenomena associated with the discovery or realization of a Christian view of the world and life, which again ultimately results in freedom. The Church's task really amounts to following the way of freedom, which is essentially a way of love. For the moment the Church has little more to do than to put into practice the freedom for which she was freed.[84]

It is not excessive to say that, for van Buren, the Church is one of the repositories of wisdom in the world, trying to contribute in thought and action to the emergence of the human world as a human place. Like Sölle he does not resolve the problem of the source of the Church's insight and power to fulfill this task. The bond and link not only of the believer, but also of the Church as such with Christ, remains vague and enigmatical with van Buren. He is thus consistent in later thinking in terms of a Church which, as a Christian society, is equated with the other "societies"—the scientific and the cultural. The Church not only has a cultural function, but she has become a cultural factor; she is one of the world's repositories of wisdom and contributes to culture not above but along with other bodies.[85]

The reader may perhaps be disappointed that, even after this description of the Church in her ethical function, he has no clearer idea of the exact significance of a secular Christian ethic. One thing, however, becomes increasingly plain. The authors in question do not develop the intrinsic nature of a secular ethic, since for them ethics is precisely the means of giving faith and the Church a place in the world and its problems. It will be left to the world itself to define the content of this ethic. To be committed to the world is perhaps the definition of a religious ethic, and this also explains not the content but the inspiration, the motive power and the aim of a secular ethic.

For all these authors, this being committed to the world, this

---

[84] *Ibid.*, pp. 191-2.
[85] According to data from Th. Ogletree, *The "Death of God" Controversy*, pp. 55ff.

relationship to the world, has a religious basis and origin—God's actions in the world, the "contagious" freedom of Jesus, the pro-existence of Christ, in short the Gospel as *kerygma,* proclamation. However, the question which is left open by most of these authors, or which at any rate is not developed and clarified, is that of the significance of this "grace-element" in a secular ethic. Their concept of the Church has not provided an answer to this question.

I shall now attempt to review this last question on the "place of God" in the various authors, in the light of the christological problem of a religious ethic.

VII

CHRIST AND A SECULAR ETHIC

One thing that always strikes and surprises me in even the most liberal discussions on the possibility of a Christian ethic is the fact that people seem able to reject God, but not the figure of Christ, no matter how he is interpreted. It is also clear, in all the authors discussed, that it is precisely their postulation of a relationship with Christ in man's actions in the world that in their eyes justifies their claim to advocate a Christian ethic. Yet wherever they establish this bond with Christ, they proceed, as it were, almost inductively from the world toward Christ.

This is in contrast to the traditional way of thinking which has Christ as its center, from whom a norm and a code of living may be imposed upon life. The meaning of Jesus (Christ) for the world is the theme which recurs as a *cantus firmus* in all secular discussions on ethics.

For Robinson, Jesus is the "man for others" in whom love has gained complete supremacy. Because Christ was so wholly and entirely a "man for others", because he was love, he was one with the Father. This love for man is also our way to God. In Jesus this love, this being for others, is revealed to us. Yet, although Robinson devotes a section of his book to the question: What does Christ mean to us? [86] and speaks of participation, the transference of Jesus' love to us never becomes clear. Robinson evidently assumes the classic orthodox concept of *unio cum Christo* (union with Christ) and wishes only to render its consequences for behavior acceptable in new terms.

Yet whenever Robinson speaks of Christ as the revelation of love, the question arises whether Christ is merely a model whom we "learn to know" or whether he is also *causa salutis*, the origin of new conduct and life. He gives his approval to a long quotation from Bonhoeffer[87] in which the latter attempts to define man's relationship to Christ in his worldly conduct. A meeting with Jesus Christ involves the discovery that here a radical change in the whole human ordinance takes place, for Jesus exists only for others; he is pro-existent. "Faith means participating in this being of Jesus." [88]

It is noteworthy that both Robinson and Bonhoeffer, and indeed other writers too, find no difficulty in accepting a "newness of life" in the world which has its origin in Christ. While there might be no problem in *ethically* defining this newness as a living for others, as pro-existence, a problem does arise concerning its origin. Ogletree rightly inquires whether, having denied any form of transcendence (vertical transcendence), it is still proper to speak of a newness which does not have its origin in man himself and in the world.

It must, however, be repeated that Bonhoeffer and Robinson are still too wedded to the theological tradition from which they, as it were, automatically derive the concepts of grace and union with Christ. They may not even realize that in this respect they are rejecting only the terminology of the traditional christology to which they are attempting to give a fresh interpretation.

Van Buren and, in a certain sense, Hamilton are even more involved in the problem of the place of Christ in ethics. Van Buren speaks of the "contagious" nature of Jesus' freedom. The

---

[86] J. Robinson, *Honest to God,* pp. 81ff.

[87] *Ibid.,* p. 82.

[88] D. Bonhoeffer, *Widerstand und Ergebung,* p. 191.

secular significance of Christ's resurrection is that his disciples had seized the experience of being through something like Jesus' own freedom.[89] Both he and Hamilton clearly state that the possibility for this self-giving love is rooted in the answer to Jesus' own freedom. Here again we find a sharing in Jesus, a transference from him to man, and yet the figure of Jesus is denied any transcendent meaning. This is where Ogletree points to an inconsistency in van Buren's thought. How can one attribute an exclusive and ultimate meaning to the figure of Jesus and expect from him the power of total change without recognizing in Jesus a reality or a dimension which transcends ordinary events and processes? When van Buren postulates the unique nature of Jesus, is he not speaking of God? [90]

The vague texts of Robinson and Bonhoeffer, to which could be added many more, and van Buren's inconsistency highlight a very real problem which is emerging in the field of Christian ethics at the present time. Kuitert draws attention to the tendency to reduce Jesus to a model understandable in historical and psychological terms.[91] Is there merely a relationship to Christ in memory of his life and doctrine, or does there exist a "presence" of Christ which supports and accompanies the life of the world? [92] Jesus' great attraction at the present time is evidently his humanity which is easy to understand and which may be expressed in practical terms and applied to the existing situation in the world. An ethical doctrine of the Gospel may be adopted and transmitted in an understandable and human way. Christ's doctrine replaces his person; religious obedience becomes support for a doctrine. But devotion to his person and union with his life form no part of a secular ethic. In any case secular ethics has compelled traditional Christian morality to face up to the

[89] P. Van Buren, *The Secular Meaning of the Gospel*, pp. 90, 128.
[90] Both Ogletree (*op. cit.*, pp. 57-8) and Kuitert (*op. cit.*, p. 143) draw attention to these inconsistencies.
[91] H. Kuitert, *op. cit.*, p. 143.
[92] Cf. C. van Ouwerkerk, "Christus en de Ethiek," in *Tijdschrift voor theologie* 6 (1966), pp. 307-17 (with English summary). The reality of the *Christus praesens* is also for Kuitert the critical moment of the whole of secular theology (*op. cit.*, pp. 152-213).

question of what it really means by union with Christ as the fundamental norm of Christian life, and what it means when it says that grace is a *lex indita*.

In the context of a Christian ethic it is just as difficult for modern man to accept God as lawgiver as to accept Jesus as the inner norm of our existence. It seemed to secular ethics that to speak of Jesus as lawgiver would be easier to understand and be immediately inspiring. But this ease of understanding is only achieved at the expense of Jesus' unique nature which forms the basis and justification of the concept of Christian ethics.

VIII

CONCLUSION

By way of recapitulation I shall attempt to summarize the motives underlying a secular, believing system of ethics, and to restate the questions which it poses for traditional morality.

The (in reality) unseen God forms the central problem of secular theology and consequently of the reality of man's relationship with God. Since man is unable to discern God clearly in this world and in human life, he rejects him as a transcendent, distant God, or else he tries to accept him as an absent or powerless God. Lacking a clearly demonstrable God, man turns to the world in order to rediscover God indirectly in the world. The mysterious reality of a relationship with God is transformed into a concrete, tangible relationship with man. Ethics, then, as the mandate of faith in and to the world, becomes of paramount importance. This ethic, too, can not revert to a God who reveals his will, but falls back upon the values offered by the world: love, liberty and humanity. In this world, however, it is possible to discern Jesus as a concrete and historical figure who may be taken as the source, model and inspiration of a free and loving existence in the world. A theological system of ethics is replaced by a christological system which, as we saw, again raises the problem of the reality of involvement with Jesus.

These more theoretical-theological questions are, however, linked with a more practical vein: the rediscovery of the world's own intrinsic value and its clear claim upon our lives and actions. Man's independence and coming of age imply at the same time the rejection of an intervening God competing with us, and the discovery of man's own ability to take this world in hand and to reform it.

God's mysterious scheme of salvation is transposed to an activity in the world which is thus not accomplished in a supernatural series of contingencies, but which becomes identical with the history of the world and with the historical tasks that the world imposes. Here, too, Jesus, who enters history, is a point of reference for rediscovering God within the world and its history. The task of Christian ethics is seen as a continuation of God's activity through a social-cultural involvement in the world.

Secular ethics considers as self-evident an optimistic view of the possibility of building up a new world and a new future. Secular ethics is imbued with a theology of hope,[93] or, perhaps more accurately, hope is the situation in which can develop a Christian form of ethics as the only reality of faith in this age of transition. Must one not speak in this interim period of a reality of God not yet present but only expected, which now, in this period, makes it both possible and necessary to live toward this future by acting ethically in the world? Between the commemoration of the historical reality of Christ and the expectation of a new world in which the reality of God will once again become visible lies the task of religion, which is called Christian ethics.

In other words, secular theology tends to seek in ethics, in action in the world, the reality of God's presence now, which is of a special nature since Christ has gone and his return is not yet a fact. This ethic is secular in its present expression, but Christian

[93] A theology of hope, which evolves into a Christian ethic of believing for the whole world is described by J. Moltmann, *Theologie der Hoffnung* (Munich, 1966); Dutch translation: *Theologie van de hoop* (Utrecht, 1966). See especially Chapter V, "Exodusgemeinde, Bermerkungen zum eschatologischen verständnis der Christenheit in der modernen Gesellschaft," pp. 280-312.

in that, looking both backward and forward, it sustains this world's link with past and future where God is present.[94] Let this be understood: we are attempting here to interpret the intentions of the secular theologians, but in so doing we think we have exposed the heart of the problem which preoccupies most of them. The fact that religion tends to become reduced to ethics is not strange in the special situation in which believing man finds himself: to be obliged to live in the world as though seeing the unseen God.

Secular ethics clearly poses certain questions with regard to traditional and especially Catholic morality. On the possibility of answering these questions will depend traditional Christian (and especially Catholic) morality's ability to withstand the pressure of secular morality. In the first place Christian ethics will have to make it clearer what is meant by basing ethics upon the will of God. We are familiar with the traditional answers, but these are evidently open to misconception. They offer modern man no "new" motive for a different (more intense, more honest or more generous) interpretation of his ethical duty.

Secondly, what role does the evangelical *kerygma* (centered about the figure of Christ) play with regard to morality? Does it merely proclaim that human behavior (which has its own inherent, unalterable norms) becomes salvation for those who believe, or has it a clear and special message for the world in an ethical respect?

Yet, even more urgent than the question of the distinctive (intrinsic) character of a Christian ethic is that of the meaning of Christ (of grace, of faith) as the ground, strength and norm of human actions. How is Christ really present in ethical behavior now? Ethics has become, as it were, a *locus christologicus* in secular theology; the *imitatio Christi* is advocated with pathos. Phrases such as participation in the life of Christ, sharing his existence and being infected by his freedom occur repeatedly.

[94] See in this connection the balanced exposition of Th. Beemer, "De Krisis van de moraal theologie," in *De Kerk van morgen* (Een postconciliar toekomstbeeld van de Katholieke kerk in Nederland) (Roermond-Maaseik, 1966), pp. 45-62.

There is an almost pathetic need for a bond with Christ. Yet the reality of this bond urgently requires a modern interpretation. Otherwise there is the danger that Christ as model may shortly stand for humanity pure and simple. Before answering "so be it", a fresh reassessment of the great christological themes of Christian ethics should first be attempted.

Finally, the pressing questions of war and birth control within the framework of Catholic morality have rendered urgent an inquiry into the ethical task and authority of the Church. From whence does she derive her ethical views and what guarantees can she offer for the solution of ethical problems? Exaggerated expectations concerning the ethical competence of the Church are indeed past history, but this renders even more urgent the question of the extent and limits within which one may and must speak of an "ecclesiastical" morality.

I have picked out only a few of the questions; there are certainly many more. They do show, however—and this was my intention—that secular ethics, certain types and symbols of which I have described, has touched upon vital questions. Fortunately, serious attempts have been made, both in Catholic and Reformed circles, to provide new answers to old, yet once again topical, problems.[95] I hope that this article will arouse a wider interest in these questions and a common desire to find the answers.

[95] We give some of these attempts here. First, there is the above-mentioned study by J. Moltmann. Next there are the ideas found in K. Rahner in various essays, collected in the sixth volume of *Schriften zur Theologie* (Einsiedeln, 1965) under the heading "Zur theologischen Anthropologie" in the paragraph "Der einzelne in der Kirche". Finally, may I list certain recent and readily obtainable publications by Dutch authors: the introduction and first part of the book by W. van der Marck, *Het Christusgeheim in de menselijke samenleving* (Roermond-Maaseik, 1966), pp. 9-46, and certain paragraphs from the book by H. Borgert, *Kerk en toekomst* (Pleidooi voor een meer wereldse kerk), pp. 127-32, 161-70). My horizon was too limited to be able to review at present other recent publications on this subject.

PART III
DO-C DOCUMENTATION
CONCILIUM

Office of the Executive Secretary
Nijmegen, Netherlands

M. C. Vanhengel, O.P./*Nijmegen, Netherlands*

J. Peters, O.C.D./*Nijmegen, Netherlands*

Signs of the Times

In the Introduction to the *Constitution on the Church in the Modern World* we read: "The Church must continually examine the signs of the times and interpret them in the light of the Gospel. Thus she will be able to answer the questions that men are always asking about the meaning of this life and of the next and about the relation of one to the other, in a way adapted to each generation" (n. 4). John XXIII had already used this expression in *Pacem in terris* to indicate the direction which the *aggiornamento* should take. The four parts of this encyclical sum up these signs of the times as so many manifestations of evangelical values which stimulate contemporary historical development from within: the emancipation of the laboring classes, the recognition of woman's place in public life, the emancipation of peoples that once were or still are colonized, universal planning, the unification of the world and the progressive socialization of various aspects of human life—aspects that are economic as well as cultural and spiritual.[1]

---

[1] M.-D. Chenu, "Les signes des temps," in *Nouv. Rev. Théol.* 87 (1965), pp. 29-39; M. van Caster, "Signs of the Times and Christian Tasks," in *Lumen Vitae* 21 (1966), pp. 324-66; J. B. Metz, "Die Zukunft des Glaubens in einer hominisierten Welt," in Hochland 56 (1964), pp. 377-91; K. Rahner, "Christ in seiner Umwelt," in *Stimmen der Zeit* 90 (1964/5), Vol. 176, pp. 481-9; G. Bortolaso, "L'uomo nell' orizonte del

1. *Signs of the Times as a Theological Source*

It is not so much the mere reference to the "signs of the times" that strikes us in these texts as the fact that they have become a source of theological development. Next to scripture and tradition, liturgy and spirituality, man's concrete existence has become a theological source. As Paul VI put it to the theologians gathered in Rome in September of 1966: "The Council exhorts the theologians to develop a theology which is both pastoral and scientific; which keeps in close touch with the patristic, liturgical and especially biblical sources; which respects the teaching authority of the Church and particularly of Christ's vicar; which is related to humanity as it is lived in concrete historical actuality." [2]

This insistence on the signs of the times is connected with another important factor in the development of contemporary theology: the acute awareness of the Church that she exists and lives within the historical process. She does not exist as a static quantity apart from the dynamic developments around her; she is *in* the world. Change, history, time and development are not external phenomena, a kind of changing decor to unchangeable man: they are part of man's inner reality. And these men are the Church. There are no two histories, one secular and one sacred. There is only one history, and this history leads to salvation or disaster. That is why the signs of the times are an integral part of the history of salvation. When the theologian tries to see these signs in the perspective of salvation, he is not just trying to be fashionable or up-to-date or to avoid "preaching" in the pejorative sense. As M.-D. Chenu has related, one of the Council fathers pointed out during the debate on revelation that tradition cannot be looked on as a deposit which preserves the past intact, as if only that past could be taken as the revealed truth; it rather must

---

tempo e dell' eternità," in *La Civiltà Cattolica* 117 (1967), n. 2775, pp. 232-40; *idem*, "Tempo ed eternità nella condizione umana," *ibid.*, n. 2785, pp. 48-55; L. Bini, "Cristo e il tempo. La teologia della Storia della Salvezza," *ibid.*, n. 2773, pp. 56-62. A good illustration of theological interpretation of a "sign of the times" may be found in I. Maybaum, *The Face of God after Auschwitz* (Amsterdam, 1965) and A. Neher, *L'existence juive* (Paris, 1962).

[2] *L'Osservatore Romano*, September 26 and 27, 1966.

be regarded as "connected with world events, with the various historical cultures in which the Church is involved in the course of events".[3] He pointed out that it was customary to point to the connection of the revelation with the concrete history of Israel, but that one should also point to the bond between the living tradition and God's guidance as manifested in later history.

2. The Implications

The signs of the times have therefore become intensely significant in contemporary theology, particularly when related to the theology of the secular. It is not every event that can be called a sign of the times. This expression, to be fully significant at all, presupposes at least two elements: an accumulation of facts that all point in the same direction and the fact that men are aware of this direction. How closely these two elements are connected can be seen clearly in the events that are related in the Old Testament. That the flight from Egypt was more than a mere escape or that the Babylonian exile was more than a mere matter of prisoners of war was realized consciously first of all by the prophet. He interpreted these events and he could do so because he saw how these events converged upon a new future, a "promised land". Chenu illustrates this with the French Revolution: "As the action of a small band of Parisian rebels, the taking of the Bastille in 1789 was relatively unimportant and similar to many other events of the same nature, but it became and was 'significant' so that for over a century it became a symbol throughout the world" (*loc. cit.*, p. 32). That Japan defeated Russia in 1918 was in itself an unimportant fact, but it strengthened the realization that the white peoples were not necessarily superior to the colored ones, and so it became a symbol of the emancipation of the colored races. It is therefore not a matter of giving an erudite analysis of an event but rather of discovering the inner driving force of a group of events which turns these facts into an enduring symbol. In this sense Toynbee speaks of history as a challenge to every culture and every religion. When a given culture or religion no

[3] F. Marty, archbishop of Rheims, at the 93rd General Session of October 2, 1964.

longer understands these challenges or can find no answer to them, it is finished, in his view. Something similar happened at Vatican Council II.

3. The Importance of Schema XIII

The discussions about Schema XIII at the Council give one hope that the Church has understood the challenge, accepted it and so created a new outlook on the future.

According to G. Philips,[4] one of the most striking moments of the Council occurred when Cardinal Suenens suggested at the end of the first session that the Church should not merely be dealt with in her internal structure but also in her relation to the world. This was welcomed with an enthusiasm that was reinforced by the general pastoral concern of the fathers and the realistic, positive and universalist view of things which animated the leaders. It was only during the debates on Schema XIII that Pope John's prophetic view of the Church's renewal came into its own. For it was not just a matter of the Church stretching out a helping hand to the world in order to make it more inhabitable, but rather of the Church's acceptance of the world's challenge and of seeing the signs of the times as an integral part of her own nature. And this took place at a time when a scientific and technical civilization was demanding more recognition for the secular world and thereby contributed to the disappearance of the sacralized world of the past.[5]

In this secular world man realizes that the key to his earthly existence lies in the humanization of this world. He knows that he is responsible for the future of humanity and that, because of his knowledge and technical ability, he is better equipped than ever before to shoulder this responsibility for the future. If we want to effect a meeting between modern man and the Church, it will have to take place in the sphere where this man takes charge of the future so that man and Church together can work out how this future can bring salvation and fulfilment.

[4] G. Philips, "The Church in the Modern World," in Concilium 6: The Church and the World (1965), pp. 5-22.
[5] J. Frisque, "Premier bilan de Vatican II," in Esprit 34 (1966), n. 354, pp. 672-4.

This vision was not yet embodied in the first draft of Schema XIII (at that moment still called Schema XVII). It was still largely a repetition of the social and political statements contained in previous social encyclicals. But if Schema XIII was to follow the line laid down by Pope John, it could not be a *doctrinal* document; it had to be, above all, a *prophetic* vision. In this connection it has sometimes been pointed out that every paragraph but one of *Pacem in terris* contains a reference to some document of Pius XII. And yet, there is great difference; a keen insight into reality turns these references into something very different from a mere application of abstract principles. Consequently, the first draft of Schema XIII showed an urge to learn rather than the clarity of a vision. Only at the last session, on December 7, 1965, was a draft submitted where the tasks of this world were recognized as tasks in their own right and at the same time as part of the work of salvation. Politics, socialization and economics are autonomous values; they have a reality of their own which cannot be dominated or doctrinally imposed by the Church.

The third world, which is now in the process of taking shape, cannot be split up into various sections but must be understood as a whole. It is this unity, this socialization, this emancipation, which the Church must learn to recognize as a sign of the times. In these sections the Church has no longer a privileged position; they constitute, as Chenu said (*loc. cit.,* p. 39), the working capital which believers and unbelievers have in common. The faith provides the convinced Christian with a kind of aerial through which he can listen in to the modern world if he abandons the doctrinaire and paternalistic attitude of the man who already has all the answers. In this way he will be able to recognize moral values, the historical actuality of which is not due to the Church, even if one admits that in fact the first impulses came from the Gospel. This is what happened with freedom, with the emancipation of dependent nations, with the place of woman in society and with the peace and unification of mankind. And so it happens with many other values which, planted in a Christian atmosphere, have become autonomous and are even launched as something new by people with an anti-Christian outlook.

In order to be truly "Church" the Church should keep away from ideologies. This is why what is important in Schema XIII is not so much the formulation as the approach with which Vatican Council II has come to accept the reality of this world as a sign of the times. Insofar as the formulation is concerned, Schema XIII was not intended to be definitive. It will have to be revised constantly, step by step, and always starting from the reality and experience of the Church in this historical world. This is perhaps the first time in the history of the Councils that such a "provisional" text is offered to all men as a service to the world.

This new awareness of her historicity and of the signs of the times did not fall out of the sky. It was influenced by a conception of "time" which derived not only from contemporary philosophy but also from a scientific study of salvation as history in both the Old and New Testaments. What Cullmann has said in his *Christ and Time* about this sense of historicity and the understanding of the signs of the times shows that this is not merely an academic matter but of extreme practical importance. Moreover, it is closer to the scriptural attitude toward history than the newness of the term would lead one to suppose.

4. *The Scriptural Background*

Lohfink has pointed out that history can be seen as repetition or as a way toward freedom. A classical culture like that of the Greeks never clearly understood this matter of time and history because it could only see history as an unceasing repetition, a circular process from which nothing new could be expected. With its unshakable trust in history as essentially the realization of the promise in the future, Israel's approach is diametrically opposed to that of the Greeks. In order to understand what is meant by the signs of the times, it might help to look a little closer into this expression.

Both Greeks and Jews put down their original historical experiences in a vast literature which survived the centuries and is still part and parcel of any civilized person's cultural possession. Blind Homer expressed the primitive experiences of the Greeks in his *Odyssey*. It is the story of man's many wanderings. Ulysses leaves home, does battle in Troy and spends his life roaming the seas. But in the end he returns to Ithaca, to Penelope, to the security of his home. He finds rest in the place he started out from; the place of his good-bye becomes the place of his final reunion. The circle is complete. History will repeat itself, and is symbolized by the serpent that swallows its tail; ritually it is celebrated in the regular return of the seasons. It is the *motif* of the constant return which permeates even the literary work of Ecclesiastes, the preacher, whose scriptural contribution shows Greek influences: "There is nothing new under the sun" (Eccles. 1, 9-10).

Israel, too, reflects on her beginnings. But here we find the opposite of that eternal return and the consolidation of the past. Abraham the pagan is called by God out of the paganism of the Amorites. He is plucked out of his home country and familiar environment to plunge into the adventure of an uncertain future. Looked at objectively, this is no more than what every nomad or gypsy does: a constant moving from one place to another. But this simple fact is seen by Israel as a *sign*. Scripture does not see this departure of Abraham as a mere adventure, but rather as the concrete expression of that faith of Abraham which is eulogized in the epistle to the Hebrews. It is seen as a first exodus. This first exodus will not only remain the model of all later kinds of exodus that occur in scripture, but also becomes an attitude that is typical of God's people. Immediately after the transition to Christianity —to "those on the way" as it is called in Acts—the author of the epistle to the Hebrews will still refer to this event as the pure and primitive form of faith: "By faith Abraham obeyed when he was called to go out to a place which he was to receive as an inheritance; and he went out, not knowing where he was to go" (Heb. 11, 8).

Abraham leaves and never returns to the oaks of Mamre from where he started. Ulysses returns to the security of his Ithaca. These two views of history show two totally different attitudes. Israel's exodus *motif,* the way ahead, shows a complete contrast with the circle *motif* of the Greeks. This exodus *motif* permeates the whole of salvation history. Even the banning from the earthly paradise, where two cherubim bar the return to the original security of Eden, shows the same idea: a departure without a possibility of return, but with trust in an obscure and uncertain future. When the Hebrew text of the sacred books was translated into Greek, this *motif* was expressed in a "technical" expression of its own: exodus. This happened in the 3rd century B.C., mainly in view of the Jews who lived in the diaspora, surrounded by Greek culture. The second book of the Pentateuch was then entitled "Exodus", a term which was loaded with religious implications.

Objectively, one might call the departure of the settled Hebrews from Egypt quite simply a "flight". But Israel saw this flight in another light by interpreting it in the light of God's presence in a calamitous situation. Does not the name "Yahweh", the name of God, imply more than a too metaphysical-sounding "he who is"? Does it not really have the connotation of "he who is present" —he who is present in a very real sense at this happening so that the Israelite never need be afraid of history, as the man of classical culture was? The same holds for various details of the exodus such as the passage through the Red Sea, the experience of life in the desert and the feeding of the pilgrims with God's manna. One after another, these facts are seen as signs of the future.

To show how this *motif* was continued in the New Testament,[6] it should be enough to point to some significant details. There are, for instance, the great self-affirmations of Jesus in St John's gospel, which remind one at once of the exodus: "*I am* the life"; "*I am* the light"; "*I am* the way"; "*I am* the bread." They are even difficult to understand in their formulation unless one remembers that passage through the desert, that column of light which led the Israelites, and the manna given in the desert. The great epiphany of Jesus on Mount Thabor introduces the heroes

---

[6] Cf. Ps. 114 and Ps. 23, 1-4. A. Gros, *De Bijbel over levenswandel* (Roermond, 1963), peruses on pp. 84 and 85 a complete parallel between the exodus and the life of Jesus as narrated by the Synoptics; St. John puts the narrative in the context of the exodus as fulfilled and achieved in Christ. Cf. J. Foliet, *La spiritualité de la route* (Paris, 1936).

of the exodus, Moses and Elijah, the prophet of the desert experience. In the Greek text, the subject of their conversation seems to be the exodus: "Two men talked with him, Moses and Elijah, who appeared in glory and talked about the 'exodus' which he was to accomplish at Jerusalem" (Lk. 9, 31-32).

This hurried survey of the exodus *motif* in both Testaments already shows clearly that this is not a mere literary *motif*. This exodus, this belief in the future, shows the pattern of life not only of the Israelite, but also of the Christian who, according to Acts, adheres to "the way". They see the history of events as salvation history. This shows how the expression "signs of the time" corresponds to the contemporary interpretation of scripture.

5. *Theological Implications*

There is a danger that these signs of the times are seen simply as some pious interpretation of events. Chenu (*loc. cit.,* p. 34) has already warned against this: "When, then, Christians, as a body, a Church, want to interpret events according to God or the Gospel, they cannot subconsciously sever them from their actual, 'worldly' reality; they cannot merely 'spiritualize' them. These events are signs in their own full and inner meaning. It is in these events, as they are in *reality,* that the Church sees something that cries out for the Gospel. These facts must therefore be respected and are not to be used for apologetic purposes. They must be listened to according to their own nature; they must not be glibly given a supernatural varnish, which leads too easily to 'mystification'."

Therefore, what has been said here must be understood in the light of the contributions by van Hulte and Chen, which follow in this issue. The depopulation of churches in Amsterdam, for example, must first be accepted as a fact and be studied sociologically. One should even extend the situation there to that prevailing in other cities such as London, Brussels, Madrid, Munich, New York, Buenos Aires, Bombay and Tokyo. As is clear from Chen's report, missionary activity cannot do without what is sociologically established in the process of the emancipation of non-white peoples if it does not want to degrade itself into a kind of spiritual colonialism. Only then can such facts be seen as signs.

To understand them a prophet may be more useful than a professor.

A few days before he was executed in 1945, Alfred Delp, a priest and sociologist, wrote in the cell of his Berlin prison: "The really great figures of history all had to pass through the solitude of the desert in order to find a new answer to the basic questions which man faces there. Only he who can face the desert can speak." He who has not gone through the desert can only repeat what he has heard others say; he can find no new meaning for old words and can discover no new words. As Heeroma put it, he not only leaves the logic of language where it is but also merely transmits the theology of the language as it was given to him by his predecessors. Then we are back in the circle movement of the classics and there will be no exodus toward freedom and the future. There is then only a plundering of the world's culture, of the *"spolia gentium,* the treasures of the pagans" (cf. Exod. 12, 33-36), but this is not the material with which to build a new altar for the worship of God.

This reading of the signs of the times is therefore in no way an easy matter for theology, particularly since these signs usually keep a certain ambiguity. What Schillebeeckx said is only too true: "In some cases there may be several solutions that are valid from the Christian point of view; in others it may be that there is only one that is morally valid and which then becomes obligatory in order to lead mankind in certain given circumstances to more human values, while this one concrete solution cannot be derived from the Christian and human norms which the Church has to put before us. Schema XIII ought to put this clearly: that the limits of the ecclesiastical hierarchy in connection with the concrete attempt to improve the world on a human basis are not necessarily also limits for the faithful who live in this world. Often it will only be history that can decide whether one or other 'worldly' decision was the fruit of prophetic witness or merely of confused understanding." [7] The two contributions which follow are meant to start the ball rolling.

[7] E. Schillebeeckx, *Wereld en Kerk* (Theologische Peilingen III) (Bilthoven, 1966), p. 137.

Matthew Chen, O.P./*Hong Kong, China*

Confessing the Faith
in Asia Today

I n the post-conciliar era, while interdenominational, inter-Church or even inter-faith dialogues and negotiations are being carried out at top levels, the importance of local and regional ecumenical developments is often overlooked or downgraded. Speaking at Enugu in 1965, Dr. W. A. Visser 't Hooft, the then secretary general of the World Council of Churches (WCC), pointed out the significance of "continental councils" as "an important link in the total ecumenical chain" between the WCC and the local grass-roots ecumenical initiatives. He referred in particular to "the very great significance of the plans made by the East Asia Christian Conference for the conference on 'the confession of the Christian faith in Asia today' ".[1]

As previously planned, the East Asia Christian Conference (EACC, founded in 1959) convened its first Faith and Order Conference in Hong Kong from October 26 to November 3, 1966, under a slightly altered title, "Confessing the Faith in Asia Today". Over a hundred delegates took part in the week-long deliberations under the chairmanship of Dr. C. H. Hwang, formerly the principal of Tainan Theological College, Taiwan. The participants came from fifteen Asian countries plus Australia

---

[1] The text of the general secretary's "Report to the Central Committee" of the WCC at its annual meeting held in Enugu, Nigeria (January, 1965) may be found in *Concilium* 6: *The Church and the World* (1965), pp. 161-70.

and New Zealand, and represented about twenty Churches, denominations or world organizations.[2] The credit went chiefly to the South Asia group for supplying the most outstanding Church leaders such as Dr. D. T. Niles (Ceylon), secretary general of the EACC, Archbishop Lakdasa de Mel, Anglican primate of Calcutta, Dr. Russell Chandran, principal of United Theological College of Bangalore, India, and Dr. John R. Fleming, editor of the *South East Asia Journal of Theology*, Singapore. Of the Geneva WCC staff present at the Hong Kong conference were Dr. Lukas Vischer, of the Faith and Order department, and Dr. W. A. Visser 't Hooft, who was then making his last public appearances before handing over the post of secretary general of the World Council of Churches.

The first EACC Faith and Order Conference had chosen a theme of distinctly missionary flavor and great actuality. The Christian communities in Asia are indeed tiny minorities scattered among the immense masses of nearly 2,000 million people, but they are, at the same time, conscious and proud of being "the first fruits of Asia for Christ" (Rom. 16, 5). The Christian communities in Asia are essentially kerygmatic communities. They are vested with the challenging mission of proclaiming the message of salvation to the Asian peoples and of confessing the Christian faith in Asia today.

Interdenominational Unity: "From Confucianism to Confusion"?

It became immediately clear, however, that as soon as Christians talk of confessing the faith or bearing witness to Christ, they are faced with the scandal of disunity among the Protestant

[2] The EACC includes the following countries or territories: Burma, Ceylon, Hong Kong, India, Indonesia, Japan, Korea, Laos, Malaysia, Singapore, Okinawa, Pakistan (East and West), Philippines, Taiwan, Thailand *and* Australia and New Zealand. At the Hong Kong consultation, the following Churches or Church bodies had sent official delegate(s): Anglican, Baptist, Basel Mission, Church of Christ in Thailand, Church of South India, Evangelical, Independent, Lutheran, Methodist, Mar Thoma, Presbyterian, Philippine Independent Church, Reformed, and a few United Churches, e.g., of Japan (Kyodan) and the Philippines. The Youth Department of the WCC, Geneva, was represented by Hiroshi Shinmi (Korea).

denominations, not to mention the divisions in the Christian family as a whole. Confessionalism stands in glaring contradiction to confession (*homologia,* consensus).

A Chinese scholar was once quoted as saying: "Christianity is leading China from Confucianism to confusion!" Many Asians would readily accept the Gospel but refuse to believe a Church "divided against herself". They would say to the Christians: "Agree among yourselves first; then come and tell us what to believe!" Church unity is a *conditio sine qua non* for an effective Christian witness: "That they may be one . . . *so that* the world may believe. . . ." *So that!* There is an inner logic at work between Church unity and its credibility. If this is true everywhere, it is nowhere more keenly felt than in mission lands. Thus the section on "Unity and Divisions" of the Hong Kong conference opened with the stringent question: "How can we confess Jesus Christ together in view of our divisions?" [3] The documents of the conference as a whole, as well as the *viva voce* interventions in the plenary sessions, struck an emphatic note of "urgency" of Church unity, and pressed the member Churches to "be prepared to experiment boldly by means of pilot projects" of unity.

Signs seemed to enkindle a cautious optimism. The Asian Church leaders generally felt that "for the Churches in Asia the overriding concern is that they should be, in spite of their different names, *identified and identifiable* (emphasis in the original) as a people together. The identity of a denomination is, in relation to this, a secondary concern". The Asians, in fact, regard denominational divisions as primarily a Western affair, and do not consider themselves bound to perpetuate the Church divisions which had arisen from historical circumstances in Europe and are of no relevance to the younger Churches in Asia today. This common feeling found an articulate spokesman in Arne Sovik (Director

[3] In this article all quotations from the minutes of the Hong Kong Faith and Order Conference are made according to the revised draft (typescript). The final version of the proceedings of the Hong Kong conference shall appear in the *South East Asia Journal of Theology* in the spring of 1967. Information is available from Dr. J. R. Fleming, 6 Mount Sophia, Singapore.

of the Lutheran World Federation Department of World Mission, Geneva). He asked: "Must we, to be Christians, become Europeans, share in the history of the Occident's quarrels and divisions. . . . ?" [4] A consensus emerged clearly: the Asian Church leaders shared a general willingness to strive for Church unity.

But considerable disagreement arose regarding how far Church unity should go. Some delegates seemed to settle for joint action for the mission, while others strongly pressed for more organic unity. During a plenary session, Dr. Visser 't Hooft rose to say: "The document is not explicit, convincing and emphatic enough on the *real* unity. The document might give the impression that what we seek for the time being is cooperation, while the real unity is not yet a discussable proposition. I must stress strongly that cooperation is *not* enough!"

The delegates also seemed to be divided on the ways by which unity ought to be achieved. Most of them, it appeared, wanted to achieve unity by means of common action, and they showed great reluctance toward dealing with the traditional Faith and Order issues. Dr. Lukas Vischer's plea for a deeper and further probing into the classical, yet still vital, Faith and Order issues, such as the Scripture-Tradition problem, along the line traced out by the 1963 Montreal Conference, failed to provoke a widespread response. The revised draft blandly admitted: "We claim no special wisdom in finding solutions" to the doctrinal problems that are still keeping the different confessional bodies apart.

Cultural Accommodation and Social Commitment: "Confessiones Asiaticae"?

"The Christian community finds itself within a particular cultural flux"; it must confess the Christian faith "from within the mainstreams of the life of the larger community in which Christians participate". That is to say, Christianity must be made

[4] A. Sovik, "Confessions and Confessing the Faith in Asia" in *The South East Asia Journal of Theology* (July/October 1966) (special EACC Faith and Order issue), p. 89.

indigenous. To this effect, indigenous forms of music, archi-tecture, painting and sculpture are welcome expressions of the Christian faith. Moreover, this process of indigenization must go further and deeper. The Christians of Asia must discover the thought-forms in their respective heritages and invest them with new meaning and new depth in the light of the Gospel. However, the section on "Culture and Community" as a whole appeared to fall short of the breadth suggested by the *leitmotiv* of the Hong Kong Faith and Order Conference, "Confessing the Faith in *Asia Today*". One would have expected it to deal more fully and thoroughly with the total problem of restating and reinterpreting Christianity in an entirely new *Zeitraum:* Asia-Today. One would almost say that the Hong Kong consultation had retreated behind the second EACC general assembly held in Bangkok in 1964. The Bangkok assembly had called for a revision of the "Christian style of living", and for a bold restatement of Christian faith "in the idiom of the indigenous cultures" after the examples set by apostles John and Paul, who did not hesitate to "press into the service of the Gospel the terminology of Greek philosophy, the symbols of the mystery religions and the structures of thought of the Gnostics".[5]

At the first EACC Faith and Order Conference, the nearest attempt at a radical restatement of the Christian faith was made not in the section on "Culture and Community", but rather in the section on "Unity and Divisions". In this section, the historical character of the traditional confessions—such as Confessio Augustana, Gallicana, Scotica, etc.—was recognized. Further-more, their adequacy was called into "radical questioning".[6] The younger Churches of Asia decided to "draw up their own con-fessions of faith and witness". The significance of this decision will become fully apparent only in the course of time.

Parallel to the need of *Confessiones Asiaticae,* there was the need of an Asian theology. Already in the Kandy (Ceylon) con-

[5] "The Christian Community within the Human Community": from the minutes, Part 2, containing statements from the Bangkok Assembly of the EACC (1964), pp. 15 and 52.

[6] *Op. cit.,* p. 73.

sultation (1965), it was felt that "the Asian Churches so far, and in large measure, have not taken their theological task seriously enough, for they have been largely content to accept the ready-made answers of Western theology or confessions".[7] A "situational theology" needs to be developed in and out of the Asian *Sitz-im-Leben*.[8] In this context it may be of interest to point out that as early as 1949, Thomas Ohm, O.S.B., the noted missiologist, had already held out the promise of a "Chinese theology" becoming the *genius* of the Chinese people. The same may be said of a theology developed with the help of Vedanta or Bantu philosophy.[9]

But a *Confessio Indiana* or *Japonica,* or even a Chinese theology, would not suffice to relate the Gospel to the Asian scene. Asian countries find themselves in the midst of rapid socio-economic revolution and political unrest. Unless the Christians have something to say about the hunger in India, or the war in Vietnam, or the urbanization in Japan, or the industrialization in Taiwan, the Gospel is for most Asian peoples utterly irrelevant, completely meaningless. Socio-political commitment is imperative. Otherwise, Christian communities would exist outside the mainstream of the Asian life and be reduced to marginal groups.

In the drafting of the sections on "Social Concerns" and on "Confessing the Faith in Politics", the two groups concerned

[7] *Confessional Families and the Churches in Asia* (Report from a Consultation convened by the EACC and held at Kandy, Ceylon, 1965), p. 21.

[8] Cf. J. Fleming, "Situational Theology" (editorial), in *One People—One Mission,* containing reports from the Situation Conferences of the EACC (1963), pp. 3-4.

[9] Cf. H. Küng, *Kirche im Konzil* (Herder-Bücherei: Freiburg im Br., 1963), p. 199: "Muss die christliche Theologie unbedingt an den Aristotelismus gebunden sein—oder kann sie grundsätzlich auch mit Hilfe einer Vedanta-Philosophie oder Bantu-Philosophie usw. entfaltet werden?" The author then quotes (p. 200) Th. Ohm: "Es mag . . . wohl sein, dass eines Tages, wie Francis C. M. Wei verheisst, eine chinesische Theologie entsteht, wie vor Zeiten eine griechische und lateinische entstanden ist, eine chinesische Theologie ganz gemäss dem Genius des chinesischen Volkes" (Th. Ohm, *Die christliche Theologie in asiatischer Sicht* (Münster/Westf., 1949), p. 47. On this whole question of adaptation or accommodation, see the book by A. Santos Hernández, S.J., *Adaptación misionera* (Bilbao, 1958), 617 pp. The author dedicates two long chapters to the cultural and philosophical adaptations (with abundant bibliography).

were confronted with a double difficulty. First, what is the Church's mission to the society? One could sense the tension between the different Protestant attitudes in interpreting the Church's social mission: "Le protestantisme, pris comme un tout, est partagé en deux camps opposés. Le premier croit à l'urgence de la transformation sociale du monde, l'autre s'en désintéresse au nom de l'espérance eschatologique." [10] With an overwhelming majority, the first tendency carried the weight. Nevertheless, there was some hesitancy in determining the theological basis for the Church's social concerns. Secondly, there was the problem of a practical nature. The political situation in some Asian countries is extremely complex. How far should the Church be involved in the political issues? Vietnam and Indonesia served as typical test cases.

Dialogue with Rome

For the occasion of the first EACC Faith and Order Conference, the Secretariat for Promoting Christian Unity in Rome sent three official observers. They were Joseph J. Spae, C.I.C.M. (Oriens Institute for Religious Research, Tokyo, Japan), Samuel Rayan, S.J. (Lumen Institute, Ernakulam, India) and José A. Cruz, S.J. (Ateneo de Manila University, Philippines). In addition, a "special guest", Theobald Diederich, O.F.M. (Studium Biblicum, Hong Kong), was also invited.[11] The Catholic observers were received with warm cordiality and took an active part in group discussions practically as full members.

The official recognition by Vatican Council II of a dialogue "on an equal footing" (*Decree on Ecumenism*, n. 9) was welcomed as a major breakthrough in the ecumenical movement. Here again, it was clear that the Asian Churches had no intention of entering into the kind of theological discussions now engaging Catholic and Protestant scholars in the West. "The dialogue," the report of the section on "The Roman Catholic

---

[10] B. Lambert, O.P., *Le problème oecuménique* I (Éd. du Centurion: Paris, 1962), p. 251.
[11] The author of this article was present throughout the meeting in the capacity of a "visitor".

Church" stated, "need not be a replica of what is beginning to happen in the West." This statement inevitably lends itself to ambiguous interpretations. It might be taken as a search for fresh approaches to the ecumenical dialogue—or as an evasion.

Other concrete possibilities, such as common translations of the bible and joint efforts in countering the force of secularism were studied, and some particular issues, such as religious freedom, proselytism and mixed marriages, were discussed. On the whole, however, the dialogue with Rome was overshadowed by the more immediate and immensely more pressing concern of interdenominational unity within the Protestant family. Before our Protestant brethren can overcome their internal divisions, the Protestant-Catholic reunion must remain perforce a remote prospect.

Michael van Hulten/*Amsterdam, Netherlands*

Pastoral Work
in Amsterdam

In 1889, when the total population of Amsterdam was 404,172, the number of people living in the city proper was at its highest (310,067). By January 1, 1955, this number had already declined to 116,825, and by January 1, 1965, there remained only 87,632 in the city proper out of a total population of 866,290, or 10.1%. It is estimated that by 1980 this number will have further declined to around 50,000. Between 1947 and 1960 the proportion of Catholics to the total population remained roughly the same, while the absolute number declined by a fifth: in 1947, 23.3% (30,297); in 1960, 23.8% (24,049). By 1980 this figure will probably have shrunk to around 14,000 registered Catholics, about 5,500 of whom could be considered as practicing Catholics.

I wish to mention here only one of the consequences of this development: the excess capacity of the churches in relation to their maximum potential usage. At the present time the nine parish churches of the city are able to accommodate 7,670, and 5,800 of these places are actually usable according to information furnished by the parish priests. Even now this number is far too high for normal Sunday use, since four to five Sunday Masses are said in each church and the number of people attending church is only 14,000. This overcapacity is expected to become even greater with the progressive depopulation of the city and the increasing decline in church attendance. This is not to mention other important factors such as the other chapels and places in the city where Mass is also said, the recently-granted facility for fulfilling the Sunday obligation by hearing Mass on Saturday evening (offered by eight of the parish churches) and the possibility that in the future the obligation to attend Sunday Mass may be entirely done away with.

It is evident that no increase in the number of practicing Catholics in the city is to be expected. The usual conclusion drawn is that some of the churches will have to close. The cost of upkeep alone, which in the last resort must also be borne by the parishioners, would seem to make such a step imperative. We are here faced with a problem that is occurring in all city areas where the population is declining, and thus in cities practically everywhere.

Perhaps the answer is that all existing church buildings should go because they are no longer located where they are most needed or because their design and structure is no longer suited to present church usage. Other churches will then be needed. Should these be smaller, less obtrusive and more closely integrated with the fabric of work and daily life? Perhaps, on the other hand, none of the churches need disappear; it might be sufficient to find another function for them within the total pastoral structure. They could be used as city churches to serve a much greater urban area.

The most obvious solution would seem to be the gradual dissolution of the parishes and the demolition of the church buildings, or at least a change in their function. This would practically eliminate any necessity for further reflection on the structure of pastoral work. A boundary is shifted and everything can proceed as before. Decisions can be taken as the need arises, such as when a parish finds its parishioners and thus its finances dwindling, or when increased dilapidation renders it necessary to pull down a church.

Such a development, however, would be unsatisfactory. It does no justice to the cohesion in all developments now taking place in

cities such as Amsterdam. The decline in population is closely
linked with changes in the housing aspirations of the inhabitants.
They want more space to live in, more light and air about them.
It is also connected with a change in the composition of the remaining population together with those who are just beginning to
take up residence, and with the growth of functions carried on
in the city that serve the entire city as well as a large surrounding
area.

It is, in my opinion, not valid to argue that the churches in the
cities must be retained for their artistic value or for their worth as
symbols. If a church is thought worthy of preservation for the
sake of art, we would do well to bear in mind that this fact alone
might be detrimental to pastoral work and also that it is not the
Church's appointed task to serve as a custodian of inherited art.
While this may once have been a valid function, it has now been
taken over by others.

Nor should the symbolic value of a church be overestimated.
The site of a church building can be of the utmost importance. I
am thinking, for example, of the church of St. Nicholas directly
opposite the Central Station in Amsterdam, the great entrance
gate to the city, or of the church of Moses and Aaron, situated
opposite Amsterdam's new town hall on the Waterlooplein and
which may well become *the* church for weddings in Amsterdam.
Empty symbols, however, are of no use at all, and among these
I include those churches which, though excellently situated as
regards "symbolic value" and the Church's "public image", are,
for all that, usually empty.

The demolition of churches and the breaking up of parishes
are, however, by no means the only possibilities. As has been
said, existing church buildings might be put to another use. They
need no longer be used, as they are now, for strictly defined parish
areas, but could be placed at the disposal of particular population groups drawn from the city as a whole or even from outside
it. The city already plays an important role as a place to work
in or to visit, and this role will probably become increasingly important, certainly from the qualitative viewpoint. Urban develop-

ment is already under way in every city and it continues to progress. If the Church wishes to show that she is part of this development in all circumstances of life, she will have to manifest this in the cities in forms different from that of the traditional parish, which is based in the main on those faithful registered as dwelling within the limits of its jurisdiction. She will have to discover new forms appropriate to the distinctive living, working and visiting milieu of the city such as have already been initiated in the "open door work", chaplaincies for foreigners, the "quarter of an hour for God", the business apostolate, youth work, student chaplaincies and no doubt in many other lesser known groups. In the ecclesiastical domain, too, the function of Amsterdam as a city then becomes plain. The forms of pastoral work already mentioned could be localized in certain churches, just as a separate place could be found for particular styles of worship (alone or in combination).

I am thinking, for example, of the students, who already meet together as a distinct group and celebrate the liturgy after their own fashion. They congregate at present in certain school chapels and, on feast days only, in the Lutheran church on the Singel, the temporary aula of the University of Amsterdam, located in the heart of the city between the seat of the rector magnificus and the university library. The artists have already taken over Ons Lieve Heer op Solder as their own church. In the same way one or more churches could be designated for the foreigners and also, for example, for the young people who often feel that the services available to them in their own parish churches in the suburbs are not sufficiently contemporary. In a number of churches the distinctive style of liturgical celebration could be orientated more toward the traditional Latin liturgy or, contrariwise, toward the modern Dutch liturgy, allowing freedom of choice to those who desire it.

This would be all the easier to accomplish in the city since the diminished population there is also changing its composition. In the city districts there is a relatively high proportion of single men and women, professional women, persons of independent means and university students. Families are normally small and births in Amsterdam are relatively low in number. If I may be allowed to generalize, the population of the city is generally of a high social level and is more mobile from a geographical viewpoint. It is to be expected that the flight from the city will involve principally the categories of complete families with growing children and the old middle classes—the "traditionals", in other words. In part, at least, the trek to the city comprises people who are lower in the social scale.

As far as the city population is concerned, changes in parish structure will meet with less opposition than elsewhere. This accords with the already established fact that the priest who looks for a parish in the city is often an "odd-man-out" in the clerical world, since the normal rules for pastoral work no longer apply in the city. It should be noted in passing that it is doubtful whether the authorities responsible for making appointments take sufficient account of the peculiar character of pastoral work among those who live in, work in or visit the city. Moreover, the church in the city will henceforth have to bear in mind that it represents there the image of the total city Church for the very many thousands who daily visit the city or who have their work there.

Just as in the whole of community life many of the most highly developed central functions are located in the most central part of the city, so also might many of the Church's activities find their culminating point there. From the administrative point of view such a system already exists in the See of the deacon in the Begijnhof. However, for the pastoral work in Amsterdam to function really well, with particular attention being paid to the problems of a big city and to the special position occupied by Amsterdam both nationally and internationally, Amsterdam would require its own bishop. A man is needed who would be prepared to immerse himself in these city problems and to impart a new aspect and a fresh vitality to pastoral work. He would have to be capable of rendering the Church acceptable again to all the people of Amsterdam, unlike now, when it is so easy to live on the margins of Church life and when for many the church buildings are scarcely more than heaps of stones, sometimes beautiful and sometimes ugly, but almost always closed, and in any event without a real role to play in the life of the city. There are many more activities which could be centralized to a greater degree and/or which should be outwardly manifested more centrally; these include publicity, planning and financing. This would at the same time release many more priests from everyday preoccupations so that they could apply themselves more to their particular task, the preaching of the message of salvation.

All this, however, would require a form of parish different from the existing ones—larger and less independent. Their size would have to be at least on the scale on which each city dweller now has experience of his own part of the city. There would be no room for the present completely independent parish priests and church centers that all too often work within their parish boundaries in mutually suspicious and stiflingly jealous isolation. There would have to be a greater consciousness of the natural cohesion that binds together various sections of the city which at Church level would have to be expressed by collaboration between Church functionaries drawn from each of the city areas. One would thus have the same structures from a legal point of view, perhaps, but in actual fact they would have received a new content.

All this demands the revision and restructuring of what has taken hundreds of years to develop. Much of this growth, in comparison with the rapid development in other domains of life, has become, as it were, ossified, and will have to be skillfully and speedily freed from this state. The Church must not dally with the stragglers but must march on ahead and take the lead so that she may be in a position to cooperate in the shaping of the community.

BIOGRAPHICAL NOTES

JOSEF BLANK: Born in Germany in 1926, he was ordained in 1951. He studied at the Universities of Tübingen, Munich and Würzburg, gaining his doctorate in theology in 1926. Among his works are *Krisis, Untersuchungen zur johanneischen Christologie und Eschatologie* (Freiburg im Breisgau, 1964).

ILDEFONS LOBO, O.S.B.: Born in Barcelona in 1936, he joined the Benedictines and was ordained in 1959. He studied in Rome at the International University of Social Studies, at San Anselmo and at the Academia Alfonsiana. He teaches moral theology at the Abbey of Montserrat, contributes to the Montserrat review, *Questiones de vida cristiana*, and is the author of *Introduccion al decreto conciliar "Perfectae caritatis"* (Barcelona, 1966).

PETER BENENSON: Born in England in 1921, he is a barrister and honorary treasurer of the International Secretariat of Catholic Jurists, as well as president and founder of Amnesty International and chairman of the Human Rights Advisory Service. He contributed a chapter on "Common Law and Natural Law" to the symposium *Light on the Natural Law* (London & Baltimore, 1964).

HEINZ-HORST SCHREY: Born in Freiburg im Breisgau, Germany, in 1911, he was ordained in 1934. He studied at the Universities of Tübingen, Berlin and Marburg, gaining his doctorate in theology in 1938. He was professor of theology at the Pedagogical College, Berlin and at the University of Berlin from 1957 to 1961, and is at present rector of the Pedagogical College of Heidelberg. His published works include *Auseinandersetzung mit dem Marxismus* (Stuttgart, 1963).

STANLEY KUTZ, C.S.B.: Born in 1932, he was ordained a priest in the Basilian Order in 1958. He studied at the University of Saskatchewan, Canada, St. Michael's College, Toronto, and at the University of Munich. He gained his doctorate of theology in 1962 and at present is assistant professor of theology and secretary to the theological faculty at St. Michael's College, Toronto. He is co-editor of *The Ecumenist*.

LÉONCE HAMELIN, O.F.M.: Born in Narcisse, Canada, in 1920, he was ordained as a Franciscan in 1949. He studied at the Pontifical College of St. Anthony in Rome and obtained his doctorate in moral theology in 1954. He is a professor at the University of Montreal and editor of the review *La vie des communautés religieuses*. Among his published works is *Un traité de morale économique au XIVème siècle* (Louvain, 1962).

COENRAAD VAN OUWERKERK, C.SS.R.: Born in Hilversum, Netherlands, in 1923, he was ordained in the Redemptorist Order in 1948. He studied in Rome at the Pontifical College Angelicum and the Academia Alfonsiana, and at the University of Nijmegen, Netherlands. He gained doctorates in theology in 1956 and in clinical and experimental psychology in 1966. He is professor of moral theology and pastoral psychology at the Redemptorist College in Wittem, Netherlands. He edited the Dutch edition of *The Law of Christ* (*Das Gesetz Christi*) by B. Häring, and is a noted contributor to *Tidjschrift voor Theologie* and *Diakonia*.

MATTHEW CHEN, O.P.: Born at Amoy (Fukien) in China in 1938, he was ordained as a Dominican in 1962. He studied at the Pontifical College Angelicum in Rome and at the University of Hong Kong. Possessing a licentiate in theology, his works include articles published in Chinese in the review *Vox Cleri, Taipei* (Formosa).

MICHAEL VAN HULTEN: Born in Djarkarta, Indonesia, in 1930, he studied at the University of Amsterdam, gaining his doctorate in sociography in 1962. He is the principal state sociographer for the reclamation of the delta of Ijsselmeer and has been granted research facilities at the University of Amsterdam. His publications include *The Catholic Church in the City of Amsterdam* in the review *Streven*, XIX (1966, No. 6).

International Publishers of CONCILIUM

ENGLISH EDITION
Paulist Press
Glen Rock, N. J., U.S.A.
Burns & Oates Ltd.
25 Ashley Place
London, S.W.1

DUTCH EDITION
Uitgeverij Paul Brand, N. V.
Hilversum, Netherlands

FRENCH EDITION
Maison Mame
Tours/Paris, France

GERMAN EDITION
Verlagsanstalt Benziger & Co., A.G.
Einsiedeln, Switzerland
Matthias Grunewald-Verlag
Mainz, W. Germany

SPANISH EDITION
Ediciones Guadarrama
Madrid, Spain

PORTUGUESE EDITION
Livraria Morais Editora, Ltda.
Lisbon, Portugal

ITALIAN EDITION
Editrice Queriniana
Brescia, Italy